EMERSON STREET COMMUNITY, A NEIGHBORHOOD CO-OPERATIVE

A Registered Project of the Living Community Challenge of the International Living Future Institute

And

EMERSON STREET HOUSE

Anchor Building for the Emerson Street Community

BY ACTIVIST AUTHOR DIANE FREANEY

Peace & Love,
Diane DF

ISBN: 978-1-957365-28-2 (e-book)
978-1-957365-24-4 (paperback)
978-1-957365-29-9 (hardback)

Author Photo by: Julie Keefe
Author Photo by: Danuta Rothschild
Architect and Engineering Consultant: Nicholas Papaefthimiou
Editor: Kali Browne
Photographer: Jen Sotolongo
Photojournalist: Julie Keefe
Project Manager: Mia Sheperd
Book Designer: Jane Lawton Baldridge

First Edition Published by Emerson House Press

For more information: the catlady@dianefreaney.com
www.dianefreaney.com

EMERSON St. HOUSE

Emerson House Press
2336 SE Ocean Blvd #230
Stuart, FL 34996-3310

Dedicated To

Nicholas Papaefthimiou - Nick's dedication and support made it possible to bring Living Building / Living Community Challenge to a happy conclusion, as the Emerson Street House transitioned to first time homeowners Nicole (aka Nikki Brown Clown) and Guillermo Sandoval and their young family in September 2022.

Basement Conversion for a Home Business (Day Care Center 520 sf). Built 2012, cost of $38,445 ($74 sf), including electric service upgrade and perimeter foundation drain for the main house.

Table of Contents

OVERVIEW OF PROJECT

After a tumultuous tenure at Florida Atlantic University (FAU) in Boca Raton Florida, I was ready for a new adventure. The LaJolla Playhouse in San Diego needed a Chief Financial Officer. I was hired and moved to San Diego. Thom Waldman local actor, was my amazing Financial Assistant.

Thom Waldman La Jolla Playhouse https://www.facebook.com/thom.waldman

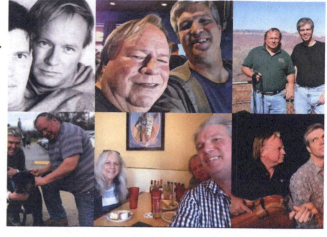

Theater is my passion; the LaJolla Playhouse was my dream job. The year was 2003, twenty years before the cracks in California's economic system are causing folks to flee California for low tax states like Florida and Texas, yet the issues were the same. I left the La Jolla Playhouse before the year was up, stopping briefly in Los Angeles to complete Cornerstone Theater Company's Summer Residency program.

Cornerstone Photo https://www.facebook.com/paula.donnelly.77

Paula Donnelly, Cornerstone's Residency Director, suggested Portland Oregon as the place doing the kind of theater I craved. After more exploring, I arrived in Portland in 2008 in the middle of a snowstorm with one suitcase and my computer and checked into a rooming house in Northeast Portland.

Third Rail Reperatory Theatre https://thirdrailrep.org/who-we-are/

Historical Prospective

My nephew Ben came to Portland on vacation. Ben is an investment guru and was studying wind and other energy resources as alternatives to oil. Ben told me that Bainbridge Graduate Institute (BGI) in Seattle, Washington was the leader in the field, granting MBAs in Sustainable Systems. Today Ben is a Realtor in West Gray, Houston Texas..

Photo of Ben https://bens.garygreene.com

BGI's Hybrid MBA held online sessions weekly with an intensive weekend at an environmental center on Bainbridge Island monthly. The terrain was difficult for an old lady with Charcot-Marie-Tooth disease, but my younger, agile classmates helped me through to graduate with my cohort.

Photo of my cohort classmates on the ferry to Bainbridge Island from Seattle.

Preface

Living Community Challenge (LCC) is Kaput

The message below appears…

Living Community Challenge is Kaput

I have spent almost a decade working on this project and now I am at the finish line, the International Living Future Institute (ILFI) says "the standard is in need of important updates and maintenance." And my work is no longer relevant?

In my opinion, this is ILFI's attempt to save face. ILFI was slow to sign up LCC projects and not one LCC Registered Project has been ILFI Certified.

I believe that Certifications are useless; actual experience is always the best indicator of success. I attempted to work with purveyors/ installers of the operating systems (HVAC, water, and electricity) but my old nemesis the company attorneys prevailed to my detriment.

Living Building Challenge (LBC) is On Life Support

A Living Building must always deal with the yin and yang of life. Once certified, the ILFI Living Building Challenge Teams go their separate ways. The ILFI case studies are never updated for positive or negative results.

The Emerson Street Building/ Community Teams are Thriving

Check out the folks who have worked on the Emerson Street Building/Community over the past decade. Most are thriving, many operate in entrepreneurial spaces, honing their skills to benefit their clients which also benefits their families and family businesses.

Prologue

COVID Pandemic Lockdowns

January 2020 brought on pandemic lockdowns as COVID-19 which began in a laboratory in Wuhan China migrated to the United States. So many problems, so many mistakes by so many elected officials and government employees who were supposed to be keeping ordinary folks safe, instead put the people they were supposed to serve in harm's way.

Work/ Live/ Eat/ Play/ Pray

Overnight everyone was told to stay home, first for two weeks to slow the spread, then indefinitely it seemed as we became prisoners in our own homes. The American people adapted with a pioneering spirit. Most folks thrived, biological families moved in together and started new businesses to pay the mortgage or rent and keep food on the table. Accidental families emerged as modern day rooming houses became one way for a homeowner to pay the bills.

Homeschooling was difficult at first until parents realized that they wanted to control what and how their children learned. The Internet became the best source for homeschooling as most school districts were slow to reorganize for remote learning.

Big Tech Became Big Brother

Big Tech responded by providing what families needed to survive, alas often at a high cost to our democratic system of government, as Big Tech used sophisticated algorithms to manipulate our minds for money.

Big Tech employees were heroes, adapting quickly to remote work, moving to rural areas where housing and other services were inexpensive, allowing Big Tech employees to keep working long hours to justify their big salaries and benefits packages.

Assisted Living and Nursing Home Residents Died Alone

Suddenly there were not enough healthcare workers, as the all folks in the healthcare field were forced to stay home with their own children abandoning their patients. Many patients had family members who were willing to help care for their loved ones, but that was not allowed.

Post COVID the World is Upside Down

Big Tech is laying off folks hired in haste during COVID. Low and middle class families tightened their belts to survive during COVID and found they liked being debt free. They also liked the home-based businesses they started and weren't interested in returning to the rat race, often with long commutes.

The layoffs post COVID are coming from the BIG companies, the Mom and Pops are thriving, often unable to fulfill all their hiring needs. The skill sets of Big Tech employees are needed by other large companies, but these companies are likely to pay half the high salaries and benefits enjoyed by Big Tech employees.

Remote Work is Here to Stay

BIG companies with BIG offices in BIG cities are having trouble luring employees back to the office. Employees got used to working from home, with a two minute commute from the bedroom to the dining room table, saving several hours daily on the train or in the car fighting traffic.

BIG city commercial buildings are feeling pinched as leases expire and tenants move out or downsize their space just as interest rates are rising. Bankruptcies are on the horizon.

The Petals of Living Building Challenge

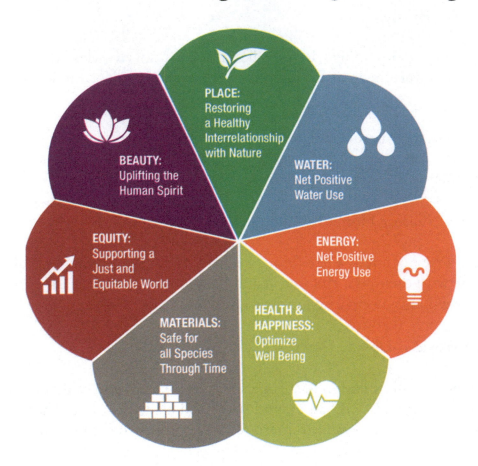

The Petals and Williams College

"The Class of 1966 Environmental Center was designed to meet the certifications of the Living Building Challenge. With under 100 current certified living buildings, the ambition of this challenge is unmatched in the world of green buildings. The LBC requires engaged participation of building occupants in the building operation, and the philosophy of the challenge is to generate good instead of mitigating harm like most other building certifications. It does so through a holistic approach to sustainability in the form of 7 petals.

Additionally, the '66 Environmental Center is designed to reduce overall operating costs to below that of the average Williams academic building, contribute to the college's greenhouse gas emissions goals, and create a green, net zero building that will attract international attention." — The Class of 1966 Environmental Center Website.

Kudos to Williams College for being among the first 100 institutions to complete the LBC. Great accomplishment for one of the wealthiest small residential liberal arts colleges in the United States, with 2,181 enrolled students in 2022. It is easier to accomplish greatness when money is not a concern.

The Petals and the Emerson Street House

The Emerson Street House Team follows a different path. We are most interested making housing affordable for lower income folks, who live paycheck to paycheck, and are always teetering on the edge of homelessness.

Energy, Water, and Materials

The three hard Petals - Energy, Water and Materials - are often the most expensive to procure and install, and seldom work as advertised. That was my experience at the Emerson Street House. I encourage you to read Append D. The ADU at the Emerson Street House, where I document the costs at less than 50% of the costs charged by ODBT.

Beauty, Equity, Health and Happiness, Place

The four soft Petals - Beauty, Equity, Health and Happiness, Place - add value to every life and are often the least expensive and most readily available. Folks everywhere discovered that during pandemic lockdowns when we were all forced to Live/ Work/ Eat/ Play/ Pray in the same space for almost two years.

A child's art project taped to the family refrigerator became a family treasure as important as the Mona Lisa by Leonardo da Vinci hung in the Louvre in Paris. The Internet became important and we struggled to make it a valued tool.

Everyone learned to ZOOM to school, church, work, libraries, theater, book clubs, etc., activities which were always in-person, became online. As the pandemic eased, folks craved in-person companionship and dynamics changed.

Some folks fell through the cracks and, as we emerged from COVID-19, we found ill-nourished families, children and individuals - physically, mentally and spiritually in our midst.

Now begins the tasks of solving the problems created by the pandemic lockdowns.

Team Bios

Marisa Zylkowski
| Sustainable Design Manager | MacDonald-Miller Facility Solutions

Marisa was Manager, Living Community Challenge for the International Living Future Institute when we met at the Emerson Street House.

From Marisa's LinkedIn page.
"In this role, I spent much of my time consulting with project teams to take a comprehensive look at neighborhood and campus development, exploring concepts of net positive energy and water, alternative transportation, health & well-being, urban agriculture and equitable place. In a typical week, I managed the program through the development of resources, providing technical support, facilitating charrettes, and delivering education."

Nicholas Papaefthimiou | AIA | infillPDX, LLC

Nicholas took over as Architectural and Engineering Consultant when the Original Design Build Team (ODBT) resigned. Nick has volunteered well over $100,000 in his time getting the Emerson Street House / Emerson Street Community back on track. I have financed three infillPDX, LLC projects, where infillPDX, LLC acted as Design/ Build, General Contractor and Landlord. Nicholas believes as I do that affordable secure housing is a human right. Nicholas pays on time so I can always count on good cash flow to finance new projects.

"Nicholas Papaefthimiou AIA is a licensed architect, developer and contractor with more than 20 years' professional experience across the United States and Europe. His experience includes work with institutional, residential, and commercial clients on projects up to one million square feet. Nicholas holds Masters Degrees in both Architecture and Structural Engineering from the University of California, Berkeley and Bachelor of Science degrees in both Architecture and Urban Planning from MIT. In addition to his professional work, Nicholas has served on multiple design and awards juries, organized and presented at numerous symposia, and served on several graduate school admission boards. He teaches courses in housing design, infill development and construction technology at both Portland State University and the University of Oregon."

Mia Sheperd
|Architectural Engineering | Block Design Build LLC

From Block Design Build LLC's web site -
From studying engineering in university [B. Sci. Architectural Engineering, Cal Poly, San Luis Obispo, 2016], working in lighting design in Portland, and then moving to Rwanda, Mia's had the opportunity to work on a range of sustainability and development work across the globe.

Mia has been designing ADUs for infillPDX since July of 2021. She recently started her own construction company, Block Design Build LLC, as a project manager and general contractor for ADUs. She is familiar with sustainable design framed by LEED, Passive House, Net Zero, and Living Building Challenge certifications as well as building with earthen materials.

Mia believes engaging the community and recognizing the history of the land, including its origins, are key elements of the success of all her projects.

Nicole Sandoval (aka Nikki Brown Clown)

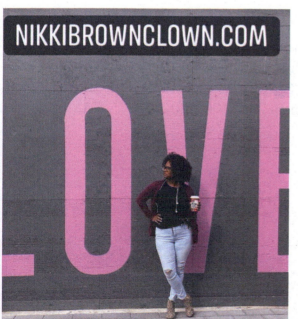

"In 2011, during the Juneteenth Parade, known as Nikki Brown Clown, she became the first Black clown in Portland. Since then, she has been active in the clown community and has earned numerous accolades. She has participated in the nationally recognized, Portland's Rose Festival Clown Corp. In 2014, she was recognized by Portland Rose Festival as Entertainer of the Year and in 2015, she was awarded Clown of the Year.

Her goal is to promote cultural pride and awareness among the Black community, with special emphasis on engaging children of diverse backgrounds. She has worked tirelessly throughout North and Northeast Portland advocating for the importance of literacy among Black children, with special attention to connecting Black children to books that support and validate Black children's experience. She started a Black Story time at a community coffee shop that ended with a Kwanzza celebration."

Guillermo Sandoval (Papi)

"Guillermo Sandoval is the CRA Director and soon to become the Financial Inclusion Director for Umpqua Bank, located in Portland Oregon. He has over 40 years in Affordable Housing and Community Development experience working with underserved communities throughout the Northwest and California. He has an economics degree from Whitman College and last year completed his MBA from Eastern Washington University. He is proud to have been chosen as the CRA Officer of the year in 2019 by the National Asian American Coalition and is honored to have his name on the Hacienda CDC Futsal Court. Outside of community work, Guillermo enjoys being with his wife and his soon to be adopted children."

Original Design Build Team (ODBT)

This is the messy part of the Living Building / Living Community Challenge. The Original Design Build Team (ODBT), has resigned from the program. It turns out ODBT was much better at gaslighting than design build so we parted company early on. Still we will be offering the original team and all original vendors right of first refusal to sign on as sponsors at $100,000 each.

LIVING BUILDING CHALLENGE
My Journey to the Living Building Challenge

In June 2013, I graduated from Bainbridge Graduate Institute (BGI) (now merged with Presidio) with an MBA in Sustainable Systems. The second-year curriculum changed the focus of my work from Wall Street investing to rooted investing – Local Living Economies (Stuart Cowan), Green Build (Jason McLennan), Energy (Jimmy Jia) and Food and Agriculture (John Gardner).

After graduation, I connected with Lise and Steve Monohan, goat farmers from Gales Creek, Oregon. Lise wrote to BGI asking for help in securing financing for a new dairy barn. Lise and Steve purchased Fraga Farms, a well-respected local goat cheese maker. The Fraga goats had to be moved from Sweet Home, Oregon to Gales Creek. Lise and Steve decide to sell their property in the Alberta Arts district.

I sold all my Wall Street investments and had cash to make local investments. Lise and I agreed on a price and closed in August.

Jeff Stern, It Situ Architecture, gave me a tour of skidmore passivhaus, his family's home, studio and office in the Cully neighborhood. Jeff built skidmore passivhaus using Passive house standards. The building is placed on the property to take maximum advantage of the sun to provide heat in cold months, electric shades to keep the sun out during hot months, thick heavily insulated walls, tight envelope, cement floors, special doors and windows.

I decided to build a Passive House, Net Zero house with an attached ADU after the tour of skidmore passivhaus. The studio and office wing has a bathroom that I wanted replicated in the Emerson Street House

Inspirations for the project were Jane Jacobs, *The Death and Life of Great American Cities*, Christopher Alexander et al, *A Pattern Language*, Annie Leonard *The Story of Stuff* and Theaster Gates, Artist, based on the south side of Chicago.

"My goal was to create community, not just build a building."

—Diane

Construction of the Emerson Street House

The Original Design Build Team (ODBT) was obligated under contract to provide visual documentation of the construction processes. EMC Charles Waylan Rogers (Chuck), Navy Seal Retired, offered to review and give me his opinion of the quality of their work. Chuck's retirement job was restoring historic buildings in California.

PROPERTY AS PURCHASED

August 9, 2013

Portland Inspections lists the probable age as 1997 (16 years old). The house was built without permits, a common practice in the Northeast Portland in the day. The garage was much older and had to come down to insure the safety of neighborhood children. The original foundation was built without rebar and the house was riddled with black mold.

DECONSTRUCTION

Looks like the garage, maybe or maybe not.

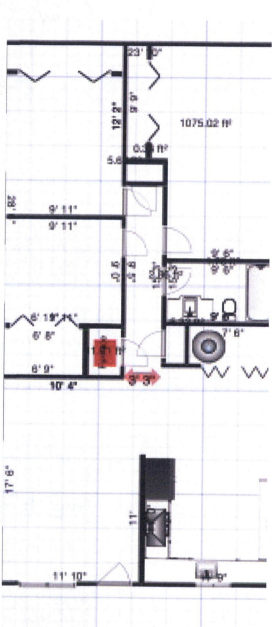

FOUNDATION

The foundation as they put the Styrofoam around the base, and then they concrete it and it helps stabilize the foundation when they put the concrete in. And I have never used this personally, but I understand how it works and apparently it is very good. And is is very, very strong and very durable.

FOUNDATION

FOAM INSTALL

And you can see where they are backfilling it with dirt. And once it's backfilled, they'll come in with the rebar for the foundation and that kind of thing, before they pour it. Then the foundation will be basically done.

VAPOR BARRIER/REBAR

You see where they've got the bracing on the outside before it's after put the vapor barriers down. It looks like number two rebar which is about one-half inch in diameter. Believe me that stuff is very strong and all of it has to be wired. Every joint where it crosses another piece has to be wired so it doesn't move when the concrete is poured.

CONCRETE POUR

Before the concrete pour, they put the dobies under the rebar. Dobies are little concrete blocks that help lift the rebar off the floor or whatever the concrete is poured over and it's pretty stout.

I don't know what the requirements are there for depth, but it's at least has to be 18 to 20 inches deep. That's hard, hard work when you start doing that kind of stuff. You got to do it fast and you have got to be good at it.

You can see where they got the plumbing all pre-plumbed around the outside edge of it. That's the PVC sticking out of the ground - the white stuff. You can see there where they are going across the top with the Styrofoam base they put around the perimeter. When they take it across there two guys and they come back, what they call screeding it with a two by four.

CONCRETE POUR

The bull float is the one who smooths it out. A lot of times, if that's going to be the floor on the inside of the house, they will come back with a power machine and smooth it out. It looks like a big fan and that really smooths it out. There's a lot of hard work, especially to get a nice straight level. You've got to do at the right time too. You can't do it too soon or too late. It you do it too soon there will be some issues, you do it too late it's not going to finish properly. But the guys that are good at concrete work, they are very good at it. When you atart doing something of this nature you have to have people that know what they are doing. If not, it will be one screwed up mess.

CONCRETE POUR

FRAMING, AIR BARRIER TIE IN

They have the framework up, using two by six walls. They do that in coal country. The insulation is thicker when it goes in. In warmer climates, like Florida, almost all the studs are two by fours. The exterior anyway they are all two by sixes or what they call five quarter nowadays, in the new language in building materials.

FRAMING

Interiors are all two by fours. You can tell where a door or a window is going. That looks like a border, that's called a header. That's where the top of a door or a window is going to be.

There's a lot of wood in that building, a lot of wood in that building. From what I can see it's being well built. They are not taking any chances on anything. They've got it all strapped down.

Down here (Florida), they call it hurricane straps. They do it from the plate to the truss. The trusses they hold things. They look like an inverted V when they are sitting on top. For those of you who don't know what a truss is, you see it being hauled down the highway on the back of a truck and has a funny looking load part of it sticking over the side of the bed of the truck.

And sometimes if it's a flat roof, you don't have to worry about that. This is a flat roof, well insulated, but it has to have proper drainage so you have to have the right pitch. And it's a two by six shelf, which you can see the insulation between the exterior and the interior.

And there are the trusses. It is amazing to me how those two pieces of punched metal is going to hold stuff together as well as they do . But they do, of course. Once it's up and the dry rock and the plywood is put on top of it for the foundation for your paper and your roof it helps hold it together as well.

There you go, They do this the easy way. They lay it down build it, stand it up and brace it. That makes it much easier rather than do it a piece at a time.

INSTALL TRUSSES

They got the floor down there and a stairwell going up. That's a lot safer than going up and down a ladder. They got a pretty good footing underneath this one with all the heavy timbers for support.

Makes a difference. Makes the home more solid, quieter, when you're walking on floors and it's a lot easier to insulate and heat. I can't tell if that is one truss of two. I think that's two one for the end, yes. Looks like three maybe.

But once they are up there they slide across the plate to get them in position. It's pretty good workers they've got on this house. They see, you know exactly what they are doing.

Spray Foam

I've never dealt with spray foam but I understand it is really quite good. They spray it in the walls. Insulating panels they put on the outside and then the inside is the same way and it just much easier to heat.

WINDOW INSTALL

I am trying to figure what he is doing with that window. Okay. It is kind of a trick to put in these windows, too, because if you don't have the opening exactly square, it could present a very big problem.

HRV-HEAT RECOVERY VENTILATION

Are those pipes in there for heat?

GREEN ROOF TPO

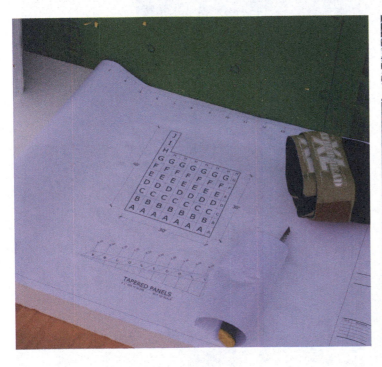

 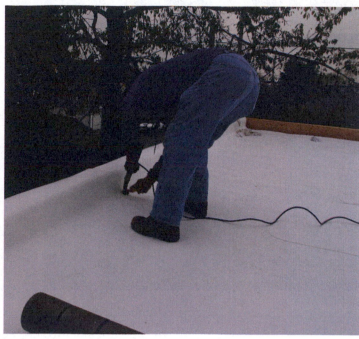

Oh I see, they are putting a green roof up there. That green border, but no you see on the outside of the building is something that hasn't been around for too many years, but it's waterproof, moisture proof so it works out very well.

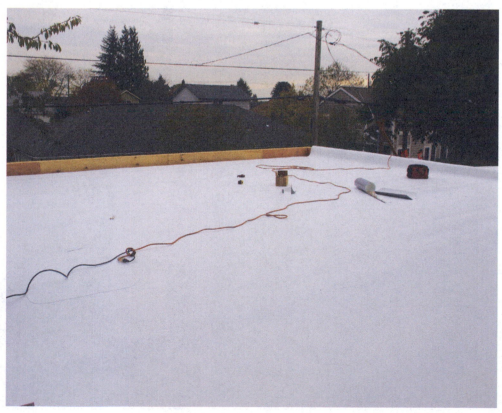

ZIP, FLASHING AND FASCIA

Then, of course, you have the metal flashing around the windows before either boarded or stuccoed.

ROOF INSTALL

Looks like they are putting a metal roof on. I personally have never been around when they installed a metal roof. I've been around a lot of tile roofs, shingle roofs. They have certain tools on metal roofs so when they nail it down they use crimps so the panels don't come apart or leak.

CORK INSTALL

It looks like cork board on the outside and the inside. It looks like corkboard but it is also insulating board.

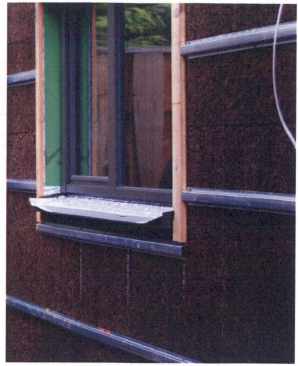

DOOR INSTALL

He's putting in the doors. Again, if the doors are not properly cut, properly built, installing a door can be a real headache, because the doors are pretty much square on the corners, and top to bottom where it closes, when the hinges are, the gap should be the same. top to bottom on both sides of the door when they are closed. Sometimes it works that way, sometimes they don't get it quite right. And it really causes a big problem for the contractor to come in and hang the doors.

PLANTER BOXES

That looks like concrete. Yeah this is concrete. Wow! They got that one well formed. They meant for that not to fall down I guarantee.

Siding Install

You know never having been on this project personally, the way it's built looks like it's done very, very well. The Contractors who did the work knew what they were doing. I look at the corners, if they were nailed together or fit together, and there are no big gaps.

METAL INSTALL

Whoever was doing the job knew exactly what they were doing. The exterior of the building looks virtually flawless. They weren't doing anything on the cheap.

BLOWN IN CELLULOSE

The cellulose that is blown in has really become very popular all over the country, especially in cold weather, cold climates I should say.

DORKS

Were they the Contractors? It looks like they
did a very good job of building the addition or
whatever they were doing.

SHOWER

If there is plaster in the bathrooms, usually what I do is put a skim coat of plaster on it like I would do stucco and then go back and put a finish coat once it's dry.

Soffit

That's pretty wood!

INTERIOR FINISHES

That must be a shower wall (above).

CABINETRY

INTERIOR STAIRCASE

That is a pretty entry way! Lights and all that.

BACKYARD

Fire Rock

Those window casings really are pretty, they did a nice job on those.

Looks like they're using ten or 12 foot pieces of rock on the inside.

Home Owners Manual

Homeowner's Manual
1006 NE Emerson St A|B

Introduction

Congratulations! Birdsmouth Construction designed and built this home to be comfortable, energy efficient, low maintenance and last a very long time. You are living in a High Performance Home that meets the PHIUS + standards and Earth Advantages' Net Zero Home, and Earth Advantages' Platinum level certifications.

The purpose of the manual is to:

- provide guidance in the maintenance of the home and equipment
- offer suggestions to improve energy efficiency
- further enhance your low - impact on the environment
- locate shutoffs to systems and utilities
- provide education about the features of this "Green" home

Please keep this manual for future use and to educate future owners of this home of the "value-added" features within. The accompanying usb drive documents all of the electrical and plumbing line locations, prior to cover, for future reference or service.

Sincerely,

Joshua Salinger, President

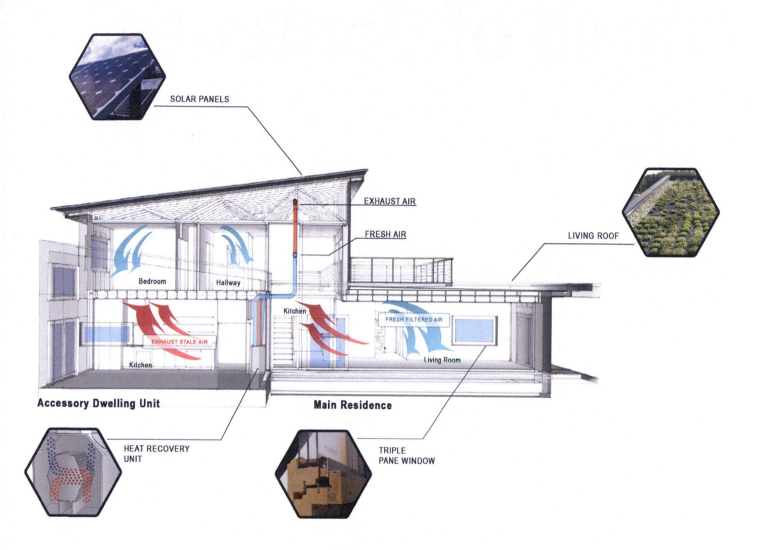

SOLAR PANELS

EXHAUST AIR

FRESH AIR

LIVING ROOF

Bedroom

Hallway

Kitchen

EXHAUST STALE AIR

FRESH FILTERED AIR

Kitchen

Living Room

Accessory Dwelling Unit

Main Residence

HEAT RECOVERY
UNIT

TRIPLE
PANE WINDOW

Table of Contents

Earth Advantage Certification

Your new home has been certified by Earth Advantage as meeting extensive green building requirements. Birdsmouth Construction used the Earth Advantage guidelines as a reference in planning and building, and has submitted documentation to show that certain criteria were met.

The Earth Advantage® Homes certification program is a third-party certification program for builders that helps them create energy efficient, healthy and resource-wise homes that add value for the homebuyer. The Earth Advantage Homes standard requires projects to achieve a minimum number of points on a scoring sheet covering five categories over the course of two verification visits, including energy efficiency, healthy indoor air quality, resource efficiency, environmental responsibility and water conservation. Depending on the number of points earned, the projects may qualify for different levels of certification: Earth Advantage Silver, Gold, or Platinum.

The standard is based on achieving required points on a scoring sheet covering five categories -energy efficiency, healthy indoor air quality, resource efficiency, environmental responsibility, and water conservation - earned over the course of two verification visits. By working with builders, designers, tradespeople, and homeowners, Earth Advantage is gradually moving the industry towards higher levels of sustainability. To accomplish this, the organization offers three levels of Earth Advantage certification: Silver, Gold, and Platinum, as well as our advanced Earth Advantage Net Zero and Net Zero Ready, Multifamily certification and our Remodel certification.

Your home has reached **EA Platinum Level** and **EA Net Zero Certification,** the highest certification levels available.

Please visit Earth Advantage's website for additional information. www.earthadvantage.org/certification/earth-advantage-home-certification

ZERO ENERGY

1006 NE Emerson Street, Portland, Oregon

May 2016

EARTH ADVANTAGE IS PROUD TO ACKNOWLEDGE THIS HOME FOR MEETING THE REQUIREMENTS
NECESSARY TO BE CERTIFIED AN EARTH ADVANTAGE ZERO ENERGY HOME.

Passive House US Certification

The PHIUS+ Certification program is the leading passive building certification program in North America. It's the only passive building certification that combines a thorough passive house design verification protocol with a stringent Quality Assurance and Quality Control (QA/QC) program performed on site by highly skilled and specialized PHIUS+ Raters. The benefits of PHIUS+ certification include:

- **Comprehensive design and energy model review**

Passive buildings in North American climates present unique design challenges; small mis-steps can lead to big problems. PHIUS+ certifiers are the most experienced passive house professionals in North America. They thoroughly review projects at the design stage, identify problems, and work with project designers to make projects work.

- **Rigorous quality assurance**

Project testing and inspections are conducted by experienced HERS Raters, trained by PHIUS to work on PHIUS+ projects. The on-site inspections and testing help to assure PHIUS and the project teams that the buildings will perform as designed.

- **Listing on the PHIUS+ Certified Projects Database**

PHIUS+ certified projects are included with pertinent project information and photos on the PHIUS+ Certified Projects Database.

Please visit Passive House Institute US website for additional information. www.phius.org

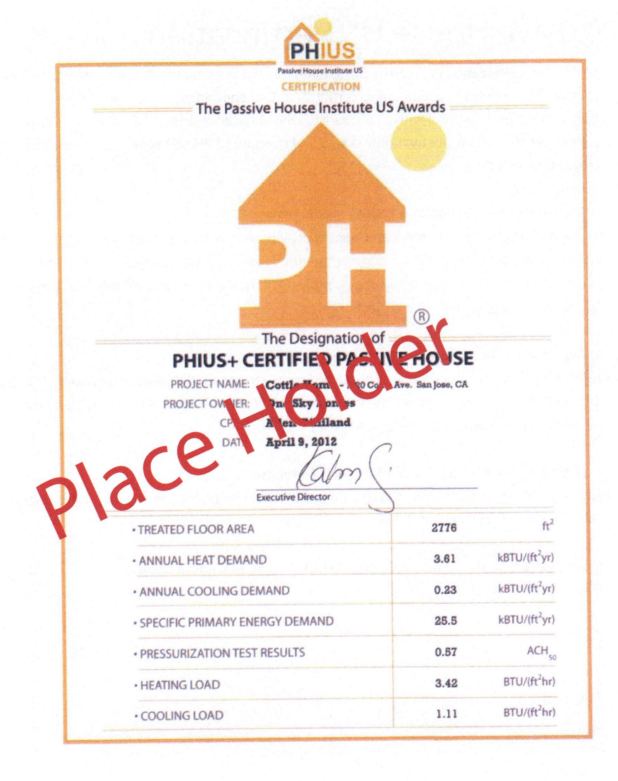

PHIUS
Passive House Institute US
CERTIFICATION

The Passive House Institute US Awards

The Designation of

PHIUS+ CERTIFIED PASSIVE HOUSE

PROJECT NAME: **Cottle Home** - 20 Cottle Ave. San Jose, CA
PROJECT OWNER: **One Sky Homes**
CP: **Allen Whitland**
DATE: **April 9, 2012**

Executive Director

• TREATED FLOOR AREA	2776	ft^2
• ANNUAL HEAT DEMAND	3.61	kBTU/(ft^{2}yr)
• ANNUAL COOLING DEMAND	0.23	kBTU/(ft^{2}yr)
• SPECIFIC PRIMARY ENERGY DEMAND	25.5	kBTU/(ft^{2}yr)
• PRESSURIZATION TEST RESULTS	0.57	ACH$_{50}$
• HEATING LOAD	3.42	BTU/(ft^{2}hr)
• COOLING LOAD	1.11	BTU/(ft^{2}hr)

Energy Performance Score

10

Energy use and carbon footprint are important factors to consider when buying, building or making energy-efficiency upgrades to your home. Both factors affect a home's operating costs, performance and impact on the environment.

EPSTM, brought to you by Energy Trust of Oregon, is an energy performance scoring system which takes these factors into consideration, making it easy to see the energy efficiency of your home. The lower the score, the better—a low EPS identifies a home as energy-efficient with a smaller carbon footprint and lower energy costs. A home's EPS can range from zero to 200+—zero being the most efficient, 200+ being the least.

EPS is a calculation—based on a range of factors—that makes it easy to compare newly built homes based on energy efficiency and expected energy costs. It helps homebuyers evaluate behind-the-walls features that affect a home's performance.

Energy score
Displayed in millions of Btu per year. A Btu or British Thermal Unit is measurement of the heat content of fuel. One Btu = the energy produced by a single wooden match.

Annual kWh + Annual therms = Annual MBtu

Carbon footprint
A home's energy consumption affects carbon emissions and impacts the environment. The carbon calculation for EPS is based on emissions from the utility-specific electricity generation method and natural gas consumption of the home.

11

brought to you by Energy Trust of Oregon

EPS is a tool to assess a home's energy cost and carbon footprint.

EPS™ is an energy performance score that measures and rates the net energy consumptions and carbon footprint of a newly constructed home. The lower the score, the better — a low EPS identifies a home as energy efficient with a smaller carbon footprint and lower energy costs.

Location
1006 NE Emerson St
Portland, OR 97211

YEAR BUILT: 2016
SQ. FOOTAGE: 2,485
EPS ISSUE DATE: 2016-06-06
RATED BY: Earth Advantage Institute
CCB #: 204173

Utilities:
Gas: NW Natural Gas
Electric: Pacific Power

Estimated Monthly Energy Costs

$27*

Estimated average annual energy costs:
$324*

Estimated average energy cost per month: Electric $27, Natural Gas $0
Estimated Energy Cost calculated using $0.1 per kWh and $0.94 per therm

ENERGY SCALE: Based on home energy use of natural gas, electricity, or energy generated from an installed renewable system.

Energy Score

12

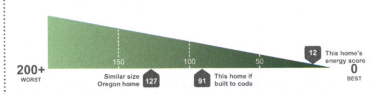

200+ WORST — Similar size Oregon home 127 — This home if built to code 91 — This home's energy score 12 — 0 BEST

Estimated total annual gross energy usage: Electric (kWh): 9,376, Natural Gas (therms): 0
Estimated average annual energy generation: Electric (kWh): 6,130
Estimated average net energy usage: Electric (kWh): 3,246*, Natural Gas (therms): 0

CARBON FOOTPRINT:
Measured in tons of carbon dioxide per year (tons/yr). One ton ≈ 2,000 miles driven by one car (typical 21 mpg car).

30+ tons/yr WORST — Similar size Oregon home 21.4 — This home if built to code 17.7 — This home's carbon footprint 3.7 — 0 tons/yr BEST

Estimated average carbon footprint: Electric (tons/yr): 3.7, Natural gas (tons/yr): 0.0

*Actual energy costs may vary and are affected by many factors such as occupant behavior, weather, utility rates and potential for renewable energy generation. A home's EPS takes into account the energy-efficient features installed in the home on the date the EPS was issued, but does not account for occupant behavior.

OFFICIAL

General Information

Optimizing Energy Use

Energy Use and Indoor Air Quality

This home has been constructed to save energy and provide comfort. Leaky homes waste a tremendous amount of energy. Well-sealed homes must have proper ventilation to maintain a healthy indoor environment.

Heat Recovery Ventilator (HRV) Unit

Ensure the filters are cleaned each season for optimal operation and comfort. The system won't have to work as hard and your indoor air will be cleaner. Heat recovery ventilators also manage relative humidity in the home and reduce heating requirements. Please see the operators manual for the maintenence recommendations for your unit, the Zehnder Novus 300.

Ventilation

The kitchen exhaust recirculates rather than exhausting to the outside. It is a good practice to use this while cooking on the stove top. Use low speed unless you need to get rid of smoke.

The bathroom exhaust and fresh air cycling fans are automatic and their operation is covered in Equipment Details & Maintenance chapter under the HRV section.

Opening windows and doors as well as utilizing fans are great for keeping the home comfortable much of the year, incorporate them as part of your heating and cooling strategy, including "night flushing" during the summer months. Screens can easily be added to the windows to keep out insects. Please contact Birdsmouth Construction if this is desired.

14

Lighting

All fixed lighting in this home are fitted with LED bulbs and fixtures. LED (Light emitting Diodes) are 90% more efficient than traditional incandescent light bulbs which result in lower maintenance costs and higher safety. Compared to 1,500 hours for incandescents, LEDs have a lifespan of up to 60,000 hours. To add some context to this see the following:

LED lifespan scenarios:
-     50,000 hours powered 4 hours/day = 34 year lifespan
-     50,000 hours powered 8 hours/day = 17 year lifespan
-     50,000 hours powered 24 hours/day = 6 year lifespan

Heating

The space heating is provided by the hydronic radiators located in select areas of the two units. The hot water is provided by the Sanden air to water heat pump and storage tank unit located in the main unit's utility closet. This system is extrememly efficient and offers quiet and clean heating that is adjustable by a thermostat located in each unit. Please see more information under the Radiant Heating Units section located on page 24.

Renewable Energy Programs

15

Pacific Power is your electricity provider for your home. For a slight additional fee, you can participate in Pacific Power's Blue Sky options which allow you to purchase renewably produced energy for a part or all of your usage. This helps build renewable power generation such as wind farms throughout Oregon. Please contact or visit Pacific Power's website for additional information

Pacific Power

www.pacificpower.net/env.html

Recycling & Compost

The city of Portland offers curbside recycling and compost on a weekly basis. Please take advantage of this, as we all benefit. Visit the Oregon Metro site for detailed information on what, how, and where to recycle.

Metro

www.oregonmetro.gov/tools-living/garbage-and-recycling

16 Disposing of Hazardous Materials

Portland Metro handles most hazardous waste for the city of Portland. They have a great online tool to list the items that you want to dispose and will generate options based on proximity of your
address.

Metro

www.oregonmetro.gov/tools-for-living/garbage-and-recycling

Alternative Transportation

TriMet is the public transit service in the Portland Metropolitan area offering bus service, street car, and Max, a commuter train service. Using public transportation means fewer miles, less maintenance and less gas for your vehicle as well as reducing pollution. For schedules and service information, visit TriMet.

Tri Met

http://trimet.org

Portland can also easily accessible by bicycle. Riding a bike to work or school is a healthy and fun way to start your day, reduces your transportation costs, and doesn't pollute. For a map of the city's bike trails and helpful tips, visit Portland Bureau of Transportation.

PBOT

www.portlandoregon.gov/transportation/article/70221

Water, Power, and Gas Shutoffs

Under normal circumstances you'll never need to shut off any of the utilities. It is always good to know where shutoffs are located in case of emergencies.

Gas

This home is gas-free. There is no supply or shut off to be located.

Electricity

The electrical panel in the Main Unit is located in the downstairs bedroom on the south wall. In the ADU it is located in the northernmost bedroom on the south wall. Be sure to familiarize yourself with this for future reference. The main breaker is at the top of each panel and will kill power to each unit. Caution ... inside the panel the power is still live. Only a qualified electrician should remove the panel.

Water

The main shut off for water is in the mechanical room of the main unit (Unit A). It is directly above the water tank on the ceiling and is labeled. This control will shut off water to both units (Unit A and Unit B) simultaneously.

Operation of Equipment

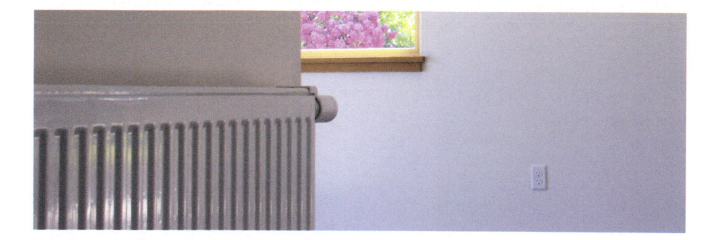

Induction Range

Your home has an induction cook range to optimize the energy usage while providing quick, safe and consistant control over the cooking temperature. Please read on for an overview of the operation and see the product manual for more in depth information.

Use the Correct Cookware Type

Cookware must be compatible with induction heating; in most models, only ferrous metal can be heated. Cookware must have a flat bottom since the magnetic field drops rapidly with distance from the surface. It is recommended to always use heavier high quality stainless stell cookware on your Induction Cooktop surface. This will greatly reduce the possibility of developing scratches on the ceramic surface.

Turning On and Off

The cooktop POWER key pad turns ON and OFF the unit. To power the cooktop ON, touch and holdthe POWER key pad for 1/2 a second. A beep will sound and the POWER LED will glow. The cooktop will be in ready mode for 10 seconds. If no other key pads are touched, the Cooktop main pwer will turn off automatically.

To turn the Main Power OFF, touch the main POWER key. A beep will sound and the Power Indicator Lights will turn OFF.

Starting and Adjusting the Cooking Zones

To start one or more of the Cooking Zones, touch the **ON/OFF** key pad for the Cooking Zone needed. A beep will sound and the selected Cooking Zone will show a dim ring of light indicating no power level for the Zone has been set.

Set the desired power level for the Cooking Zone by 1 of the following methods:

Method 1: Slide a finger in the the ring touch area. Use the "6 o'clock" position as the lowest heat position and rotate clockwise for increased temperature.

Method 2: Directly touch any position in the ring touch area (such as "12 o'clock" for medium)

Method 3: Touch "-" and/or "+" pads for precise power value.

IMPORTANT OPERATING NOTES:

- Fluids spilled or objects lying on the controls area of the cooktop may cause the cooktop to display an error code and turn OFF while cooking. Clean spills or remove the objects from the cooktop.
- Be sure the cooktop vent openings are NOT blocked, the cooktop internal sensor may shut off the cooktop to avoid overheating the appliance.
- If the cookware or pan is moved from the center of any active Cooking Zone for any reason, a sensor will detect the situation and the cookware will no longer heat. The affected Cooking Zone display will rotate the LEDs surrounding the digital display indicating a pan is not detected. The Cooking Zone will remember the power level setting for up to 34 minutes before the Cooking Zone will automatically shut off.

Care and Cleaning

Damage to the ceramic glass cooktop may occur if you use an abrasive type scratch pad. Only use cleaning products that have been specifically designed for ceramic glass cooktops.

For light to moderate soil:

Apply a few drops of cooktop cleaning cream directly to the cooktop. Use a clean paper towel to clean the entire cooktop surface. Make sure the cooktop is cleaned thoroughly, leaving no residue. Do not use the towel you use to clean the cooktop for any other purpose.

For heavy, burned on soil:

First, clean the surface as described above. Then, if soils remain, protect your hand with a potholder and carefully scrape soils with a metal razor blade scraper, holding scraper at a 30 degree angle to the surface. Remove loosened soils with cooktop cleaning cream and buff surface clean.

For additional information and troubleshooting, please see the Electrolux EW36IC60LS product manual .

22 Radiant Heating Units

Your home is equipped with hydronic radiant wall heaters to provide space heating in each unit. This is an extremely energy efficiaent method for heating your home in conjunction with the air tight building assembly and the insulation package installed. The following information is available to assist the homeowner with adjusting the temperature.

Adjusting the Temperature

Unit A: The main unit (Unit A) has two wall radiators, one on the lower level across from the bathroom, and the second in the upstairs hall. Both of these radiators are turned on & off by a single thermostat located at the bottom of the stairs. The thermostat does display the temperature of the units at the device.

Unit B: The secondary unit has a single wall heating unit located in the main hallway and is also turned on & off by a thermostat which is located in the hallway near the laundry doors.

The wall thermostats in each unit are solely used as an on/off control - not to adjust the temperature. To change the temperature up or down It has a temperaure control unit directly on the radiator that can be dialed for adjustment. The following table provides an approximate guide for the temperature:

Thermostat Sensor Head Setting						
Dial	*	1	2	3	4	5
Approximate Room Temperature °F	40	57	63	68	73	79

Please Note, unlike a typical home with forced air furnaces, Passive House homes tend to take slightly more time to heat to move up or down and is normal behavior for these types of building assemblies.

Heat Recovery Unit (HRV)

A Zehnder Novus 300 HRV system has been installed to supply continuous fresh air from the outside into the home. The heat recovery core of the unit transfers a portion of the heat in the stale air being exhausted to the fresh incoming air from the outside before being distributed throughout the house. The result is a continuous supply of fresh air, without unpleasant drafts, and increased comfort for the home occupants.

Filters

The Zehnder Novus (F) 300 ventilation unit is fitted with class G4 filters (Merv 7/8) as standard for outside air and extract air. An optional F7 pollen filter (MERV 13) is available for outside air.

Control and Operation

The ventilation unit is controlled and operated using the control unit, which is located in the main closet of Unit B. The high-quality TFT touch panel with colour display and intuitive user guidance provides the means for control and operation via a touch screen and optimises communication with the ventilation unit.

Temporary Ventilation Boost

A temporary ventilation boost button is located in each bathroom and kitchens of both units. This provides a quick, advanced exhaust of air from these areas for 15 minutes from normal operating speed. Use this feature as you would any typical bath fan to remove steam or odors from your bathroom or if you need a quick flush from cooking. This unit is extremely efficient and thus quiet, so it may not be audibly apparant that the unit is in the 'boost' mode. The HRV will automatically return to its normal operating mode at the end of the 15 minute cycle.

24

Maintenance

To maintain the Zehnder Novus (F) 300, users simply have to change the integrated filters in the front of the unit regularly (every 6 months) and visually inspect the heat exchanger. The heat exchanger should be cleaned at least every 2 years (more often if it gets very dirty). This can be done by simply removing the heat exchanger (the hexagon shaped item) from the device and cleaning it with soapy water. Please see the unit manual for additional servicing tasks.

For replacement filters please contact Small Planet Workshop:

www.smallplanetworkshopstore.com/zehnder-novus-300-g4/

Please read your owner's manual for more additional information and optimal operation.

Condensing Dryer

A Blomberg heat pump dryer has been install in both Unit A and B. Instead of a traditional vent to the outside of the home, this dryer drains any moisture via a drain. Heat pump dryers recirculate warm air, removing moisture as the clothes tumble. These units are extremely efficient while offering easy maintenance.

Maintenance

The only difference between this dryer and a traditional model is that your unit has two lint traps. The normal lint trap is located in the usual location, right in front of the drum. To access the second lint trap, push a botton on the front of the dryer to unlock the covered door.

Red indicator lights on the control console will remind you to clean the secondary lint trap every few cycles, as long as you're paying attention to the dryer display, everything should be fine.

26 Windows and Doors

The handle on the sash operates the tilt-and-turn hardware of the windows and doors. There are three positions of the handle that trigger three different modes of operation:

1. **Handle pointing down (default position):** The window or door is locked. The mulitpoint locking hardware locks the operable sash into the frame in multiple locations.

2. **Handle pointing sideways (horizontal):** The operable window sash or door leaf can be turned to open inward for cleaning or ventilation purposes. To close the operable window sash or door leaf, turn it back into the frame and turn the handle to the default position (handle pointing down).

3. **Handle pointing up (vertical):** The window or door can be tileted in. Turn the handle up and pull lightly to tilt the operable window sash or door leaf inward. To close, tip it forward, push it into the frame, and turn the handle to the default position (Handle pointing down). When operating large units, please use your other hand to push the operable window or sash or door leaf into the frame securely before and while operating the handle.

Please see the Tanner Windows and Doors Owner's Manual for additional information and maintenance instructions.

> Do not change the handle position if the window is open. This may result in the multipoint hardware to not engage properly.
>
> It is not advised to leave any door or window in the fully open position unattended. Strong bursts of wind may suddenly slam open or close a window, which can potentially damage the unit; not to mention startle you unexpectedly.

External Shades

The Emerson St. house is equipped with Hella external shades on the south side of the building in both Unit A and B. These are an integral piece of equipment for this home to assist with climate control - especially during the summer months. Understanding the function of this product will greatly assist with the comfort level of your high performance home.

Control and Operation

The shades are mechanically operated by remote which has been provided with this home. To move the blinds up or down, press the bottom most button until **all** the circle lights are illuminated. Then press the up or down button for the direction you want the shade to go and then touch the "stop" button to stop. To rotate the blinds, press the bottom most button until the circle light comes on in the upper left corner. You now can press the up or down buttons to tilt the blinds. When you want to stop the motion, press the "stop" button.

When to Use

Close the shades on hot, sunny days - this is especially true during the shoulder seasons (the time just before summer and again just before fall). A hot day in spring or fall has the most potential to allow heat into the house; conversely, please open the shades on cool gray days if additional heat is needed. In a nutshell, down in summer, up in winter. As you become more familiar with the behavior of your home, you will become more attuned to the desired operation to maximize its potential.

Be aware that during extreme strong winds it is highly advidsed to close the blind to the up position to avoid inadvertant damge. If the blinds are frozen solid, do not operate or force the blinds into another position, wait until they defreeze and then operate as normal.

28 Photovoltaic (PV) Panels

This home has 24 solar panels to meet the energy goals and make this a net zero home. With minimal maintenance, you can ensure that you will get the most out of this equipment.

Cleaning

It is recommended to clean your solar panels twice a year, in spring and autumn, to remove any debris, pollen, or other objects that might reduce the effectiveness of the solar panels to capture solar energy.

- Solar panels can be incredibly hot in sunshine. Either clean your solar panels in the morning /early evening, or pick a relatively cool day.

- First try using your garden hose to clean your panels. If a lot of dust and dirt has accumulated, then you might need to clean more thoroughly.

- Fill a bucket or spray bottle with warm water and soap. Use a soft brush or sponge attached to an extension pole to lightly scrub each panel clean - never walk directly onto a solar panel!

Take extra caution if cleaning the solar panels yourself.

Consider hiring a professional solar panel cleaner to do the job if you don't feel comfortable working on the roof

Landscape Design

Landscape Management for Low Maintenance and Enhanced Biodiversity

The key to low maintenance and ecological maintenance is to use a light hand on the landscape, and only intervene when it is really beneficial to do so. Rather than controlling the landscape you are gently coaxing it in a certain direction. Think of it as 'light' maintenance.

Imagine the conditions that the plants would encounter in their wild homes, and try to mimic those conditions in your yard. West of the Cascades this includes the accumulation and decomposition of organic matter on the surface of the soil. By allowing a natural accumulation of leaves and dead plant matter in shrub beds, you provide opportunity for a rich diversity of life forms to exist and you also shorten your chore list. For example, beneficial insects lay their eggs in dead plant stems, and beetles and worms that break down leaves also provide food for foraging songbirds. As the plant matter decomposes it also helps your plants by returning nutrients to the soil, protecting plant roots from extremes of hot, cold, and drought, soaks up rainwater and so reduces storm water runoff, and contributes to the build-up of carbon in the soil.

32

TREES
CASCARA (RHAMNUS PURSHIANA) 1.5" CAI
VINE MAPLE (ACER CIRCINATUM) 5-6' HT
STARLIGHT DOGWOOD (CORNUS X. 'STARLIC

GROUNDCOVER:

(v) —— INSIDE OUT FLOWER (VANCOUVERIA HEXAN

(Ct) FOOTHILLS SEDGE (CAREX TUMULICOLA)

(Ad) —— MAIDENHAIR FERN (ADIANTUM PEDATUM)

(Iris) OREGON IRIS (IRIS TENAX)

(aq) —— WESTERN COLUMBINE (AQUILEGIA FORMOS

(hm) SMALL LEAVED ALUM ROOT (HEUCHERA MIC

(a) DWARF GOLDEN SWEET FLAG (ACORUS GR,

(t) THREE LEAF FOAMFLOWER (TIARELLA TRIFOLI

(tr) TRILLIUM (TRILLIUM OVATUM) (3 PLANTS PER

SHRUBS :

(P) WESTERN SWORD FERN (POLYSTICHUM MUNITUM)

(Ga) SALAL (GAULTHERIA SHALLON)

(Vo) EVERGREEN HUCKLEBERRY (VACCINIUM OVATUM)

(Mr) CREEPING OREGON GRAPE (MAHONIA REPENS)

(Av) KINNICKINNICK (ARCTOSTAPHYLOS U. 'VANCOUVER JADE'

(Fg) DWARF FOTHERGILLA (FOTHERGILLA GARDENII)

(Vp) RED HUCKLEBERRY (VACCINIUM PARVIFOLIUM)

NE EMERSON ST.

(3) ACER
CIRCINATUM
MULTI. 5' MIN HT

(1) RHAMNUS
PURSHIANA
1.5" CALIPER

PLANTER PALETTE: (TO BE DETERMINED, SEE IMAGES)

(En) RED BELLS ENKIANTHUS (ENKIANTHUS CAMPANULATUS 'RED BEI

(Ln) DWARF LEUCOTHOE (LEUCOTHOE FONTANESIANA 'NANA')

(m) CREEPING WIRE VINE (MUHLENBECKIA AXILLARIS)

(Ac) SWEET FLAG (ACORUS GRAMINEUS OGON)

(H) WINTER JEWELS LENTEN ROSE (HELLEBORUS X. HYBRIDUS)
'PAINTED DOUBLES, GOLDEN LOTUS, WHITE PEARLS, ROSE QUA

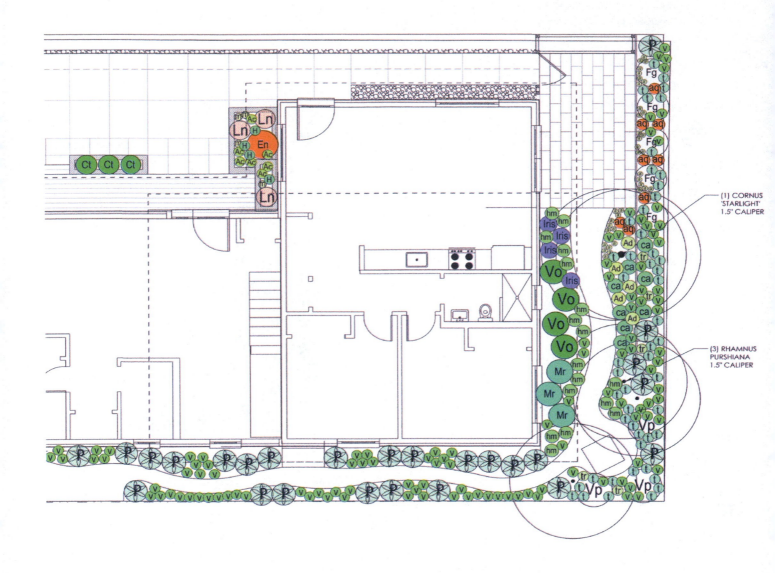

(1) CORNUS
'STARLIGHT'
1.5" CALIPER

(3) RHAMNUS
PURSHIANA
1.5" CALIPER

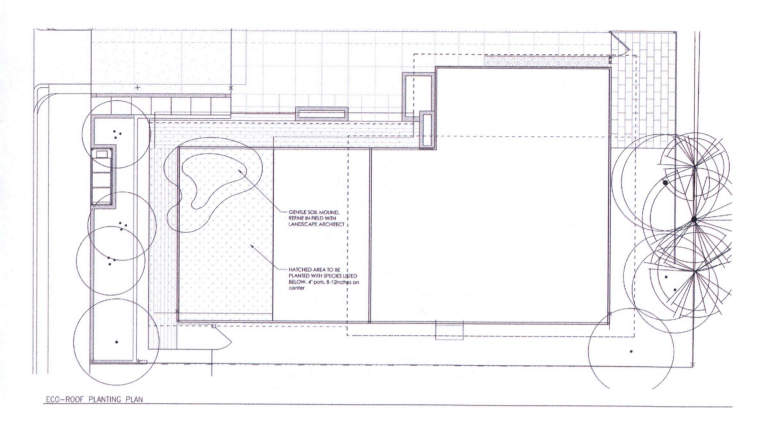

ECO-ROOF PLANTING PLAN

PLANT LIST

NATIVE YARROW (ACHILLEA MILLEFOLIUM)

BLUE-EYED GRASS (SYRINCHIUM BELLUM)

SHOOTING STAR (DODECATHEON HENDERSONII)

NODDING ONION (ALLIUM CERNUM)

WILD FAREWELL TO SPRING (CLARKIA AMOENA)

DOUGLAS MEADOW FOAM (LIMNANTHES DOUGLASII)

OREGON SEDUM (SEDUM OREGANUM)

PACIFIC SEDUM (SEDUM DIVERGENS)

ROSE SEDUM (SEDUM LAXUM)

ROEMER'S FESCUE (FESTUCA IDAHOENSIS V. ROEMERI)

CALIFORNIA POPPY (ESCHSCHOLZIA CALIFORNICA 'COASTAL FORM')

OREGON SUNSHINE (ERIOPHYLLUM LANATUM)

PEARLY EVERLASTING (ANAPHALIS MARGARITACEA)

SPREADING PHLOX (PHLOX DIFFUSA)

SEA THRIFT (ARMERIA MARITIMA)

BLUE GILIA (GILIA CAPITATA)

BLUE VIOLET (VIOLA ADUNCA)

LICORICE FERN (POLYPODIUM GLYCYRRHIZA)

580 SF @ 12"-8" O.C. = 670-1500 PLANTS. SEE PLANT SCHEDULE FOR SPECIFIED SIZES AND QUANTITIES
NOTE: ECOROOF PLANTS TO BE PLACED BY LANDSCAPE ARCHITECT ON-SITE.

ECO-ROOF PLANT LIST

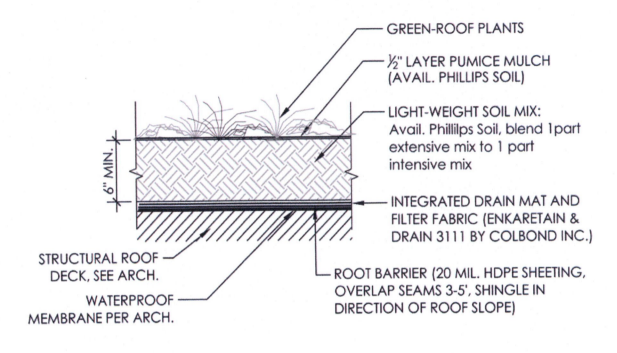

GREEN-ROOF PLANTS

½" LAYER PUMICE MULCH
(AVAIL. PHILLIPS SOIL)

LIGHT-WEIGHT SOIL MIX:
Avail. Phillilps Soil, blend 1part
extensive mix to 1 part
intensive mix

INTEGRATED DRAIN MAT AND
FILTER FABRIC (ENKARETAIN &
DRAIN 3111 BY COLBOND INC.)

ROOT BARRIER (20 MIL. HDPE SHEETING,
OVERLAP SEAMS 3-5', SHINGLE IN
DIRECTION OF ROOF SLOPE)

6" MIN.

STRUCTURAL ROOF
DECK, SEE ARCH.

WATERPROOF
MEMBRANE PER ARCH.

ECO—ROOF SECTION

TREES

Key	Latin Name	Common Name	Cont. Size	Qty	Native?
	Rhamnus purshiana	Cascara	1" cal	4	y
	Cornus x 'Starlight'	Starlight Dogwood	1.5"cal	1	
	Acer circinatum	vine maple	5-6' ht	3	y

SHRUBS

Key	Latin Name	Common Name	Cont. Size	Qty	Native?
Av	Arctostaphylos uva-ursi 'Vancouver Jade'	Vancouver Jade Kinnickinnick	1 gallon	5	
En	Enkianthus campanulatus 'Red Bells'	Red bells Enkianthus	5 gallon	1	
Fg	Fothergilla gardenii	Dwarf Fothergilla	5 gallon	5	
Ga	Gaultheria shallon	Salal	1 gallon	4	y
Mr	Mahonia repens	Creeping Oregon Grape	2 gallon	11	y
Ln	Leucothoe fontanesiana 'nana'	dwarf fetterbush	1 gallon	2	
Vo	Vaccinium ovatum	evergreen huckleberry	5 gallon	4	y
Vp	Vaccinium parviflorum	red huckleberry	5 gallon	3	y

PERENNIALS

Key	Latin Name	Common Name	Cont. Size	Qty	Native?
aq	Aquilegia formosa	western columbine	4"	8	y
hm	Heuchera micrantha - native green	small flowered alum root	1 gallon	17	y
H	Helleborus x. hybridus Winter Jewels series	Lenten rose	4"	4	
Iris	Iris tenax	Oregon iris	4"	5	y
t	Tiarella trifoliata	Western Foamflower	4"	50	y
tr	Trillium ovatum	wake robin	4" or bulbs	15	y
v	Vancouveria hexandra	inside-out flower	4"	168	y

FERNS AND GRASSES

Key	Latin Name	Common Name	Cont. Size	Qty	Native?
a	Acorus gramineus 'Minimus'	Dwarf golden sweet flag	4"	36	
Ac	Acorus gramineus ogon	Golden sweet flag	4"	7	
Ad	Adiantum pedatum	Maidenhair Fern	1 gallon	5	y
ca	Carex deweyana	Dewey's sedge	1 gallon	8	y
Ct	Carex tumulicola	Foothills Sedge	1 gallon	15	y
P	Polystichum munitum	Sword Fern	1 gallon	35	y

seasonal bloom

Feb	Mar	Ap	May	Jun	Jul	Aug	Sep	Oct	Cultural/Aesthetic Features	Habitat Features
		▓							Neutral understory filler, leaves nice from below	butterflies, berries for birds
		▓	▓	▓					Large creamy-white flowers. Red fall color, orange fruit. Good disease resistance.	Flowers- bees, butterflies. Birds like fruit.
	▓	▓	▓	▓					Small pink flowers, good fall color	bees, early bloom

seasonal bloom

Feb	Mar	Ap	May	Jun	Jul	Aug	Sep	Oct	Cultural/Aesthetic Features	Specific Habitat Features
	▓	▓							Pink or white flowers, often winter foliage color	Bees, hummingbirds. Birds like berries
		▓	▓						Delicate shape and flowers, fall color	
		▓	▓						Honey-scented blooms, orange fall color	Bees
		▓	▓	▓	▓				Evergreen, dense cover against weeds	early nectar flowers, berries later, dense cover
	▓	▓	▓	▓					Evergreen, shade/sun, yellow flowers	bees, birds
		▓							Edible berries	birds like berries
		▓							Edible berries	hummingbirds and bumblebees, berries for birds

seasonal bloom

Feb	Mar	Ap	May	Jun	Jul	Aug	Sep	Oct	Aesthetic Features	Habitat Features
		▓	▓	▓					Bright red & yellow spring flowers	Butterflies, hummingbirds
		▓	▓	▓					Tough, evergreen, good filler, airy cream-color flowers on red stalks	
▓	▓								Evergreen foliage, later winter flowers like jewels	
		▓	▓						Bright blue flowers in spring. Grass-like foliage	Bees
		▓	▓	▓					Evergreen foliage, cream-colored spring flowers	
▓									Bright white spring flowers	
			▓	▓					Semi-evergreen. Small white summer flowers.	

seasonal foliage

Feb	Mar	Ap	May	Jun	Jul	Aug	Sep	Oct	Aesthetic Features	Habitat Features
▓	▓	▓	▓	▓	▓	▓	▓	▓	Small evergreen grass, bright color	
▓	▓	▓	▓	▓	▓	▓	▓	▓	Medium evergreen grass, bright color	
		▓	▓	▓	▓	▓	▓		Delicate deciduous fern, likes moist shade. Blue stems	
		▓	▓	▓	▓	▓	▓		Pleasant green blades for shade to part shade	
▓	▓	▓	▓	▓	▓	▓	▓	▓	Semi-evergreen tufts, thin blades	
▓	▓	▓	▓	▓	▓	▓	▓	▓	Evergreen, adaptable	Low cover for ground birds

PERENNIALS & ANNUALS- GREEN ROOF

Key	Latin Name	Common Name	Cont. Size	Qty	Native?
	Festuca roemeri	Roemer's fescue	4"	270	y
	Achillea millefolium - white	Yarrow - native variety	4"	36	y
	Allium cernum	Nodding Onion	4"	36	y
	Anaphalis margaritacea	pearly everlasting	4"	18	y
	Armeria maritima	Sea Thrift	4"	18	y
	Clarkia amoena	Clarkia	Seed or 4"	36	y
	Dodecatheon hendersonii	Shooting Star	4"	36	y
	Eriophyllum lanatum	Oregon sunshine	4"	36	y
	Eschscholzia californica 'Coastal Form'	California Poppy	Seed	1	y
	Gilia capitata	Blue Gillia	Seed or 4"	36	y
	Limnanthes douglasii	Meadow Foam	Seed or 4"	36	y
	Phlox diffusa	Spreading Phlox	4"	18	y
	Polypodium glycyrrhiza	Licorice Fern	4"	36	y
	Sedum divergens	Pacific Sedum	4"	36	y
	Sedum laxum	Rose Sedum	4"	36	y
	Sedum oreganum	Oregon stonecrop	4"	36	y
	Sisyrinchium bellum	blue-eyed grass	4"	36	y
	Viola adunca	Blue Violet	4"	36	y

seasonal bloom

Feb	Mar	Ap	May	Jun	Jul	Aug	Sep	Oct	Aesthetic Features	Habitat Features
			■	■	■	■	■	■	Airy white flowers, long bloom period, naturalizes	broad variety of insects
				■	■	■			Summer-blooming	Butterflies, bees
			■	■	■				Silver foliage, drought tolerant, adaptable	butterflies
		■	■						Bright pink flowers over tufts of grass-like foliage	bees
			■	■					Annual, bright satiny flowers late spring-early summer	Bees, especially native bees
			■	■					Bright pink spring flowers	
			■	■	■				Drought tolerant, yellow blooms	variety of pollinators
			■	■	■				Summer bloom, bright orange	bees (honey, bumble, sweat, etc), butterflies
			■	■	■				Annual. Blue flowers over a long period in summer	bees, butterflies
			■	■					White spring flowers	Bees
		■	■						Purple flowers, rock garden plant	Bees
■	■							■	Cool season fern	
				■	■				Evergreen, red foliage in sun. Yellow summer flowers	bees
				■	■	■			Rose colored flowers all summer	bees
■	■	■	■	■	■	■	■	■	Groundcover plant in rock garden	butterflies
	■	■	■						Small purple flowers, spreads easily	bees
		■	■						Blue spring flowers	Bees

Seasonal Guidelines for Landscape Maintenance

40

Plan to water for establishment during the first 2 summers, and continue to keep an eye on plants during summer heat waves. Deep and less frequent watering will encourage deeper root growth, which means more drought tolerance in the long term. A soaker hose woven between the plants and attached to a battery or wind-up timer can be an easy way to irrigate landscape areas.

Plants to watch for drought stress even after establishment include:
- Anything in a planter, including concrete planters at front door & plants behind the retaining wall in the back yard
- Fothergilla
- Enkianthus

Fothergilla

Enkianthus

Annual Service Calendar

Spring

Clean gutters of debris

Check glass doors and windows - seals, caulking and exterior paint. Replace or paint as needed.

Perform building inspection to ensure systems are operating properly; test electrical systems for fire hazards, check plumbing and possible water damage areas.

Inspect the roof for damage and/or leaks; repair if necessary

Check interior paint and repaint when necessary

Check smoke, carbon monoxide, and radon detectors for proper orientation. Be sure to clean the units as needed.

Visually inspect exterior grills of HRV unit to ensure no debris is blocking the intake or exhaust grills

Clear gutters of debris.

Clean Solar Panel array of pollen, debris etc.

Summer

Replace air filters on HRV unit

Clean window and door tracks

Make sure to not overload extension cords or surge protectors

Monitor indoor humidity to maintain 60% humidity or less.

Make periodic checks of storage areas, backs of closets, etc. to be sure no oily rags, unvented gas cans, painting supplies, or flammable cleaning materials have been forgotten. These items could be a fire hazard and should be discarded.

Autumn

Check glass doors and windows

Inspect all doors and windows for proper operation and a tight fit

Check smoke, carbon monoxide, and radon detectors for proper orientation. Be sure to clean the units as needed

Inspect the roof for damage and/or leaks; repair if necessary

Perform building inspection to ensure systems are operating properly; test electrical systems for fire hazards, check plumbing and possible water damage areas.

Perform a safety inspection of your home, inside and out, to discover problem areas; check stairs, steps, handrails for sturdiness and reliability.

Clear gutters of debris and prepare for the winter rain season.

Clean Solar Panel array of pollen, debris etc.

Winter

Remove hose connections and store hosse to avoid freezing

Replace air filters on HRV unit

Check caulking around all showers, sinks, and other plumbing connections

Check for leaks around all plumbing connections and make necessary repairs.

Visually inspect exterior grills of HRV unit to ensure no debris is blocking the intake or exhaust grills

Check all connections in your electrical system to correct any possible hazards

Additional Information

Items listed below are areas that might need a little extra attention, or at least common knowledge for future reference.

Permeable Concrete

If you haven't noticed, the concrete in the driveway has a slightly different appearance than standard. In order to meet the requirements for permeability of water on this lot, permeable concrete is utilized. This allows water to pass directly through the surface in order to reduce runoff from the site while recharging the groundwater. In order to keep the permeability of the concrete operating at a high level, <u>use a regular garden hose with a spray stream</u> to clear any dirt or debris. **Alternatively**, <u>vacuuming</u> rather than sweeping the concrete is the recommended method for removing small particulates that have settled in between the aggregate.

Air Admittance Valves (AAVs)

Air admittance valves are negative pressure activiated, one-way mechanical valves, used in a plumbing or drainage vent system. As with all drains, ventilation must be provided to allow the flowing waste water to displace the sewer gas in the drain and then to allow air to fill the vacuum which would other wise form as the water flows down the pipe.

These valves should typically last up to 20 years, but if for some reason you have issues with drainage, clogs, or sewage smells, the valve may be faulty and need replacement. Your home has an AAV near each sink and each laundry area. They are located in the wall covered by a slotted grill. <u>To replace</u>, simply unscrew the existing AAV and replace with a new one.

Typical AAV

Arc Fault Circuit Interrupters (AFCIs)

AFCIs are designed to detect and respond to potentially dangerous electrical arcs in home wiring. This home has AFCIs in the circuit breakers in the electrical panel of Units A and B.

An AFCI might activate in situations that are not dangerous and create needless power shortages, but under normal operating equipment this should not occur. If for some reason power has suddenly stopped from an outlet, check the electrical panel located in your respective unit and find the associated breaker that has been tripped and reset it.

Your Home Air Barrier

The air barrier of your home is the boundary that separates the indoor (conditioned) air from the outdoor (unconditioned) air. This is an essential component of Passive House construction that assists with the durability of the home and assists with moderating temperature fluctuations. In a home such as Emerson St., creating a tight air barrier minimizes the amount of air leaks that can bring in cold air during the cold months and hot air during the summer. Ensuring that the air barrier stays intact is extremely important to long term comfort of the occupants and durability of the home. The following guidelines will help assist you to make sure you (or future home repair persons) don't accidently penetrate this portion of the structure.

- Never drill into the exterior siding or cladding. The air barrier lies approximately 3" behind the wood and metal siding. You could safely staple to the wood if needed, but penetrating a screw or nail into the siding is a risky move and should be avoided.
- If a modification is needed, please contact Birdsmouth Construction or any other certified passive house builder to assist with your needs.

WHAT IS THIS PLACE?

Conversations around the Emerson Street House

table of contents

contributors

Heather-Mariah Dixon | design

Wynde Dyer | images

Diane Freaney | interview

Julie Keefe | interview, images

Laura Lo Forti | quote

Neighbor on Emerson House Street | quote

Nicole Sandoval | interview

Donovan Smith | interview

Erica Thomas | editor, interviews

Introduction by Diane Freaney

The Certificate of Occupancy for the Emerson Street House was issued in May 2016. We immediately started planning on how to introduce the Emerson Street House to the Portland Community. Erica Thomas, Works Progress Agency, signed us up for Design Week Portland 2017.

We convened a group of Emerson Street Neighbors to design our presentation. Emerson Street was in the Northeast Quadrant, a low income historically black neighborhood, an area with no other homes on the Design Week Portland 2017 Tour.

What could we do to entice folks to go out of their way to visit the Emerson Street House? We decided to go with…

what is this place?

Erica helped us produce a small blue book called What Is This Place?, which we would give to folks who ventured up to Emerson Street. We expected a small group, but they would be the adventurous types - "our people."

a note from the editor

I first noticed Diane as a fellow outlier during a presentation I was giving at the 2016 Alliance of Artist Communities conference. I was on a panel among five other women who had all developed "self-declared artist residencies." Diane came, as she often does, to listen. At the end of the session, I vaguely remember her raising her hand and saying, "I'm not an artist, I'm a finance person. I want to know how I can support these kinds of projects." At the time, I was quite nervous to talk about this self-legitimized component of my work, in which I declare development of relationships to be part of my art practice. I came to understand later that this presentation has had an ongoing impact on her. Once we met, it became clear that we had a shared understanding of many things, and that we had some work to do together. So we began to meet and have conversations about her project at the House, which planted the seeds for this publication. Many people have asked us, What is Emerson Street House? Rather than tell you what the place is about, we thought it would be best to turn the question outward, to those who are doing the work, and listen to the response.

- Erica Thomas

"There is love in our community. Thanks to everyone who came out to paint the
Nikki Brown Clown Free Library Mural last week. Looks like we will be doing more painting soon."
- Muffie Delgado Connelley

Q & A with Diane Freaney
Owner/Founder of Emerson Street House and Erica Thomas

How did you get to this place?

I bought the house from Lise and Steve, goat farmers, who needed the equity of the house to build a barn for their goats. My daughter said, 'Mommy, the house doesn't look like you.' But, for the first time in my life, I wanted to be rooted.

I went to a reading of Cottonwood in the Flood on Memorial Day 2015, the anniversary of the Vanport flood, which wiped out the second largest city in Oregon. I learned that many long-time Portland residents were just learning the history. Folks who had lived in Portland for 20 years had never heard of Vanport. I realized that being rooted involved much more than purchasing a house.

Nikki Sandoval (aka Nikki Brown Clown) spoke of meeting you at Elevated Coffee, through an introduction by neighborhood 'elders,' as she put it. She was, and still is, touched that you wanted to honor her by naming the library after Nikki Brown Clown, and feature her in the mural on the front of the house. How does your experience of meeting each other speak to the methods you are using to develop the Emerson Street House?

I met Joanne through the Emerson Street Garden. We began meeting on Fridays at Elevated Coffee. Elevated is the neighborhood place to meet friends, check e-mail or conduct business. Joanne introduced Nikki one Friday. I met Nikki as Nikki Brown Clown during story time at Happy Cup Coffee Shop.

As we talked, I saw how important she was to the local community and I knew she was getting married and moving to California. I suggested a Nikki Brown Clown Free Library, which quickly became 'The Parade of Children' mural on the wall in front of the house. Nikki was a single mom who raised four children in Northeast Portland and she was the architect of the rich culture of the neighborhood. It felt important to me to honor Nikki for her work.

The process for creating materials and evolving the public face of Emerson Street House has been a collaborative one. We first connected after attending a panel at the Alliance of Artist Communities on social practice art residencies.

How has learning about community- based art influenced you?

After a long career in finance, I was bored to tears, but not even remotely interested in retiring. I discovered community-based art and began to feel alive again. I just have to let go of control and LISTEN. Once I started it was easy and so much more fun.

How did you select Julie Keefe's "Messages to a President" as the first public art exhibition at Emerson Street House?

Donovan knew Julie Keefe from a local news publication, The Skanner. We invited her to bring her exhibit, which was first prepared for the Oregon Historical Society, to the Emerson Street House. Julie's work is all about everyday people living ordinary lives in North and Northeast Portland. I was so honored that Julie allowed us to have her exhibit here.

Donovan is such a core part of the Emerson Street House. How did you know you wanted to bring him in initially as the artist in residence, and how did he become the Director of the DIY Artist-in-Residency Program?

Donovan was a facilitator at a Portland Alliance of African- American Leadership Circle meeting. Donovan was young, smart and his own person, which I admired. In December, Donovan needed a place to live; at the same time I had this crazy idea to start a DIY Artist-in-Residency Program. Donovan spoke about 'activating the space.' He is full of fresh new ideas—ideas not even in my frame of reference.

Diane fluffing up pillows for Joanne's Quilt and Pillows

Joanne's Quilts

Created by *Joanne Green*

My quilts, goes back four generations. My ancestors were African-Americans. Having been raised on a small farm in Texas, my inspirations for quilting comes naturally.

My quilts are made from scraps of fabric. The fabric is mostly cotton. Without a pattern, I piece together different colors. I love to see the beautiful colors blend. I sometimes surprise myself with the finished look.

As I sew, I listen to music and enjoy a good cup of coffee. I find satisfaction and pleasure making quilts, wall hangings, pillows and framed fabric art. My quilts are far from perfect, but they are unique. Yes, they are one of my inspirations. Yes, they are one-of-a kind.

"We Expect Too Much of New Buildings,
and Too Little of Ourselves."

- Jane Jacobs, urban studies author and activist

Interview With Nicole Sandoval
Nikki Brown Clown, Interview by Erica Thomas

How did you become Nikki Brown Clown?

I am very much a Portlander. I graduated from Roosevelt High School and went to community college in Portland. I had been working in early childhood education, but I wasn't happy. I couldn't put my finger on it. But my factory worker mom…she was not going to be excited about me saying I want to be a clown.

I was working for the county and my job was to go to culturally- specific events to solicit people to sign up for resources. Folks weren't coming to my table. I mean, who wants to come to the table and self-identify as being low income? Then I got this invitation from my aunt to do an event as Nikki Brown Clown. I asked my boss if I could hand out materials from the county there. We were promoting free lunch in the park at that time.

She said they would have to pay me, but she thought it was ingenious. I gave away rolls and rolls of stickers, as opposed to letting them sit on the table. That's when it hit us…the awareness went way up. People couldn't get enough of her. But I didn't want the county to own the character. Eventually, I started to make my weekly wage on the weekends at birthday parties. And I had fun! It didn't feel like work.

One of the things that gave me my street cred, my 'cultural competency,' [laughter] was being part of the Black Parent Initiative. They contracted me for the Colorful Families program in 2014/2015. I give them credit. Once I did that, people at the county library started asking for me, and it took off from there.

Can you tell me about her character?

Nikki is my nickname. And the children used to say, 'Did you see that brown clown?' so they gave me 'Brown Clown.' At first I was fighting it, but it was catchy. Sometimes clowns do this whole whiteface

118

and they hide their identity or ethnicity. I decided I wasn't gonna do that. I leave a lot of my brown skin showing. I had a lot of folks say, 'Hey, you're not supposed to do that, you're supposed to cover up!' And I said, no, I'm gonna roll with it. Nikki started to be the face of the black community, so to say. Portlanders trust her. I am a community clown...an approachable clown. That's why people like her. But it took a while to sell Portlanders on. Especially black Portlanders.

What do you think the resistance was?

First of all, nobody wants to be wrong. You don't want to call somebody out if that's the way they were dressing, you know. And no one had seen a black clown, let alone a black female clown. We've also been told that clowns are bad. Nobody had a preconceived idea of what a cute clown would be. Some people's characters are covering up, using whiteface, and are completely different. But my character is a real character. She's what everybody wants to see. I had to train Portland to accept me, to say, 'I am a clown and this is what a clown does.' It was really interesting.

Everybody's like, 'Portland's being gentrified'...And everybody has their own way of dealing with it. Some people will be like, 'I'm gonna go picket or I'm gonna go shut this down'...But I'm a clown, and there's nothing challenging about me. So people can ask me questions and kind of watch and learn. Basically, I use Nikki Brown Clown to help me cope with it.

Reflections Bookstore, they used to be the only black-owned bookstore, and they closed. The black community was really upset about it. A new shop opened and a lot of people were going to boycott it. And the sad part is that they actually had a good purpose. It was Happy Cup, and they employed a diverse group of people, with different abilities. And so I used my platform of Nikki Brown Clown, and asked, 'Could I do a story time?' But I also educated the owner. She had no idea when she leased the place that it had been formerly a black-owned business. Through the story time I was able to bridge the community together and create a diverse spot. For a year I offered free story hour every Tuesday. It's how I filled the void of me not finishing school and becoming a teacher. I was able to teach diversity and tolerance in those hours.

Story Time with Nikki brown Clown at the Emerson Street House

I think what's interesting about Emerson Street House is that we are asking people, including ourselves, to think more critically about the roles we play in gentrification and community. When I first met Donovan [Smith] I saw on some level that Diane got it, that she understood. There's an openness.

Yes, everything you're saying is stuff that I've had in the forefront of my mind. I'm very protective of my brand. It's not so much about me making a lot of money it's about [Nikki Brown Clown] being responsible. I have to be very careful what she touches because people trust where she says to go.

I lived on [Diane's] street and I remember walking past her house being built, and I was really frustrated thinking, Who the hell is gonna live there? What type of person is going to be there? At that time I lived in low income, affordable housing at the end of the block. It's interesting to think about all this work I was thinking this person might move in and not have any attachment or any goals for assimilating into the neighborhood and I was quite wrong. In my mind I lived in the worst house—the cheapest house—on the block. And now my face is on the 'baddest' house on the block! [laughter]. And then I was the first person to stay in the front part as an artist-in- residence. I was really touched.

How did you and Diane finally meet each other?

At Elevated [Coffee], on MLK, that's my favorite shop to have my meetings...I walked in and Diane, Joanne [Suell Green] and my other neighbors, were there together. They knew Diane, and they said 'Hey, Nikki Brown Clown! Come over here, I wanna introduce you to Diane.

We're over here brainstorming about this library Diane wants to do and I suggested that she should put Nikki Brown Clown's name on it. Everybody loves her. She's all about literacy!' I hadn't really put it together, but I had dedicated a lot of hours to story time at Happy Cup. Diane said, 'Yes, that makes sense, we should honor her work at the library.'

I still didn't get it, I just thought she was another lady, and Joanne told me which house she lived in and I said, 'You mean that bad house over there? Ohhh, okay.' So then that took the edge off. I can't be mad 'cause I envisioned a whole different type of person. I found out it was two units.

Then Donovan came into the shop and Diane already knew him. So then that gave her a little bit more street cred in my mind. I had heard about Donovan just from being around Portland. They said, 'Well, if you're not busy, let's walk back to the house. It's still under construction but would you like a tour?' That right there blossomed, that made me like her, because to me there's nothing like—and Diane still has that approach-'How about right now? Let's do it right now.' Not, 'Let's think about it.' Not,' Let me get your phone number and do a background check.' You know? If two or more people said Nikki is the business, she was sold on it. Joanne is an elder. I thought that was beautiful that these elders said Nikki was cool.

Neighbors Alaia (left) and Georgye (right) painting the mural at Emerson Street House

So we went back and looked at the house. I literally was in tears. I was crying. I was like, Wow. I had always wanted to be either a teacher or a librarian, so to have a free library dedicated in my name, oh, I was there for it. Absolutely. I mean, that was just, it was just beautiful. So that's kinda how that relationship happened.

And Diane did not let me go. Even though I told her I was moving to California, she did not care. She gave me a place to stay. She's kind of like a motherly figure to me. Whatever she said she was gonna do she would do it. That was it.

Whatever I need, she has my back.

I know she loves you. She talks about you all the time. Everything you're saying mirrors my experience with her. She's such a connector. She brings people in.

Definitely. That's her.

And I knew Donovan from his project Gentrification is Weird and I had been watching on Facebook how that all unfolded. There's a lot of stuff I would be interested in as a Portlander. You know how you have that list in your head?

Totally, I have a list too!

I have a whole secret list! Brown Clown has made it easier to fulfill. But it was interesting to find out that he already knew about me and the stuff I do. It makes me feel good to know that he recognized me as a change agent.

People...people have this idea of what white people should do when they move into the neighborhood to not just be a straight-up gentrifier. Everybody says, 'They should go and meet the neighbors, and they should do this and that.' Well, the crazy part is that Diane actually did that. So many people are used to

Nicole Sandoval (Nikki Brown Clown) and Guillermo Sandoval (Papi) at the Emerson Street House

people not doing it that they make this assumption that she didn't. So, when you get to know Diane you realize she actually did way more than you probably did.

Even though the Emerson House is structured, she brought me and Donovan in to still bring that community feel. And that's why people were scared of it, because it had a name. It had business hours. But Donovan and I and Joanne, we bring that down home feel. I mean, you have to have structure, but at the same time we made sure that it's still a home. It's still community. Because Diane's white, she gets that skepticism.

It's a hard balance between things that feel nice, and respectful of the community, but not so polished that people won't want to engage with it at all.

Yeah. It takes time, because it's like with any kind of relationship, you know, whether its friendship, marriage or a partnership. It takes time to get that trust. Even though I put my name on it, and I have ties to the black community, people have to find their way.

This interview has been edited and condensed for publication.

Robin Corbo Muralist working on her mural at the Emerson Street House

Joanne Suell Green paints Nikki Brown Clown's green wig at the Emerson Street House

I have fond memories of our coffee times at Elevated, when Diane was Planning what she wanted Emerson Street House to be-
Best was the day Joanne Greene introduced us to Nikki Brown and the free library was born around the table, amid smiles, stories, hugs and tears that come from being heard.

- A Neighbor and friend of the Emerson Street House

Conversations with Donovan Smith & Julie Keefe

Julie Keefe is an artist, photojournalist, and long-time Portland resident. In 2012, she was named the city's first Creative Laureate. She became the first artist to exhibit at the Emerson Street House gallery in 2017.

Donovan Smith, the first Director of the Emerson Street House Gallery, curated her show, "Messages to a President" in March of 2017. He is the founder of a line of clothing, Ignorant/Reflections, and uses his art to create conversations about gentrification in North and Northeast Portland.

The 56-year-old Keefe and 25-year-old Smith met to discuss their work together at Emerson Street House on April 1, 2017 at Locale on Mississippi Avenue, in Portland, OR.

Julie: I was always curious how you started writing for [historically black, local Portland newspaper] The Skanner. I went to school for journalism but I was always interested more in photography. I just started hanging out with photographers and submitted my work to Willamette Week. And then a job opening came at The Skanner, and I was in no way a certified photojournalist, but they gave me a chance and I just learned on the job. I was curious about you because you followed a similar path as I did. Where did your skills as a journalist come from?

Donovan: Yeah, I went to Oregon Episcopal which is considered one of the best schools in the state. I was always being encouraged in my writing by teachers and my mom, Laverne Ballard. She is a super awesome writer, multidisciplinary artist. My mom is one of those artists who's never put her work out there, but she's a great poet, she's a wordsmith and visual artist. When I went to college that was never a part of my thinking, that I'm about to become a writer. I wasn't doing a lot of studying or anything. [laughter]

Julie: But you had that great education. What did they tell you were good at?

Donovan Smith introducing Messages to a President during the opening of the exhibition

Donovan: They told me I was a good writer, I was good with history. But I never pursued it during that time. I was not trying, really at anything, when I was in high school. But they told me I had an eye in my art disciplines. I remember the very first time I heard about screen-printing and I was like, so excited, that you could take an image and put it on a T-shirt. That was amazing.

When I was in college, I took a creative writing class and I wrote a story about how my mom hit this dude who would always be walking around our neighborhood. He'd walk by on 42nd, never say anything. One day, we were all at my mom's house, and that dude ran across the street and said 'You goddamn nigger!' to my mom and pulled back to...to hit her. She was outside pouring chicken grease from the skillet, and she hit this man upside the face with the skillet!

Julie: Oh my goodness!

Donovan: Yeah! None of us kids heard or saw it, but when she came in she was super frantic. That memory will never leave me. And so I wrote a story about that for my creative writing class and my teacher told me, 'You should consider publishing this.' At that time I was probably 19.

Julie: Wow, that's like, the beginning of your memoir, right? You probably wrote other self-reflective pieces before that.

Donovan: I hadn't actually! That was the first time I ever considered that my work could be published. Eventually, I showed The Observer [an historically black, local Portland newspaper] a few creative writing and opinion pieces, and asked if I could start writing, and they asked me to go on assignment.

Julie: How long were you at The Observer?

Donovan: About a year and a half. It wasn't a long time.

Julie: That's longer than you were at The Skanner though. It's interesting that you worked at both places.

Donovan: So...I got fired from The Skanner. I have a history of getting fired. [laughter]

Julie: Did you get fired at The Observer?

Donovan: I did. That one happened because, well, when [protests] started happening in Ferguson [Missouri] I mostly ignored it at first. Ferguson is one of the oddest things that's happened... because of the military response the night [Michael Brown] got murdered—they brought all these police municipalities to this town that's almost the equivalent of Gresham. Why would you bring state police, military police, and city police to this small town with these protesters and point guns at them? It doesn't make sense. And why was his body picked up in a blacked-out van, not a medical van? And why was it four and a half hours? None of these things make sense to me.

When I saw these things on the live streams I was blown away. There was a call...they were looking for journalists. I was like, I have to go out there. And so I gave The Observer super short notice that

I wanted to go. I said, 'I can do a story on this.' And they said, 'We already covered it.' There was this protest on MLK. And I said, 'That's not the same thing. This is a moment in our history. I think it's important.' So I cranked out a bunch of stories for them that night. They told me, 'If you go out there you might not have a job when you come back.' I went out there and when I came back I got fired.

Julie: That's pretty ironic, isn't it? That you leave to cover one of the biggest national protest events of your adult life that's happened in the United States . . . It lasted a week...

Donovan: I think it lasted two weeks.

Julie: And then you get fired from a traditionally black paper.

Donovan: Yeah, I mean...It hurt me... It hurt me for a lot of different reasons. But it was also part of the necessity of my trajectory. Not to sound like Dr. Cornel West or something. [laughter]

Julie: So then after Ferguson you get hired by The Skanner...

Donovan: Yeah. Right after I got fired I did this Gentrification is Weird exhibit, which I had already been planning before I got fired. I wonder if they knew about my creativity outside the newsroom. The community at large seems to know that I'm a creative person.

Julie: I never saw your show, where was that?

Donovan: It was at this nonprofit gallery, c3:initiative—through the grace of Sharita Towne, another artist here in Portland who's been doing a lot of good work around gentrification. I was just like, 'I'm gonna do an exhibit, and I'm gonna do it in two months, and I don't have a space, and I don't have money.' And Sharita offered like, this is how you're supposed to do it, and made that whole project possible, and helped me

Julie: Sorry I missed it!

Donovan: No, it's all good... [laughter]

Julie: I've been thinking a lot about why I call what I do 'art' and I think it's because it allows people to participate. So your work interests me because you didn't come from a journalistic background. You just had a wake- up-call when you saw Ferguson and you had to go. I think that motivation is something we share.

"Your exhibit defines the community outside of the sadness of it all."

Now, I want to focus on your curatorial vision for the Emerson Street House. At this point I'm more interested in how the next person is going to fit into that puzzle. And how you're gonna keep growing this place that develops conversation, asks questions, and helps connect people.

Donovan: You reached out to me when you heard about me coming into the position as Director. And I'm grateful that you did. I didn't know where I was gonna start curating the gallery. I had some loose ideas. The fact that you had just had your exhibit at the Historical Society and you were willing to bring it into this space without having even seen it. That was really dope.

Julie: It's gonna sound ridiculous to use this word but I was, I don't know, desperate to get the show into this community. I wanted it to be in a place where it could create conversations around it, rather than a place that people just walk through.

Donovan: In a lot of ways that was supposed to be the first exhibit, that was meant to be at the Emerson Street House. I really believe that. I think that was a moment of definition for what we're going to become. We're in the heart of Northeast Portland, in the heart of gentrification. Your exhibit defines the community outside of the sadness of it all. The sadness is present but it's not the focal point of the exhibit. It's a part of life just like it's a part of life still if you're black in Portland. I just love that we started there.

It's important that you had so many people from your community show up. I went out into the community and knocked on doors to let people know the show was happening. And we had actual neighbors show up, and people from other spaces that showed up. I think we did a lot of things right.

Julie: That must feel good!

I was super charged with being able to record people who came by delivering their message to the president. As well as get everybody who was there to get in conversation with each other while they waited to have their portrait made. I think that vehicle taught us something about being able to get people to connect at a gallery opening. You're bringing people together from all different sectors, I guess.

Is that part of your vision?

Donovan: Yeah, outside of the physical art on the walls, I'm curating the vision, in collaboration with, of course Diane, but with the community at large. That's the thing about your exhibit. Beyond opening night it's been great for a lot of people.
I think the artists are gonna be a mix of newcomers and established people. But prioritizing people who come with a view that community is a pillar of their work.
I think that has to be the ultimate thing.

Julie: You're looking at a holistic response to community. Trivia night, hip hop chess, spoken word, participatory art, even thinking about creating conversation around affordable housing. But it all focuses back on...how would you say it?

Donovan: Re-visioning community.

Julie: Yes. I've been thinking a lot lately about the night President Obama was elected. The main historically black paper—The Skanner—decided to go to a digital-only edition on Thursday after he was elected. That decision blew my mind. All the elderly community, who didn't have access to computers at their home, couldn't hold that paper in their hand. It was this diminished view of our first black president, made by the editorial staff and the publisher of The Skanner newspaper. It blew my mind. Ever since then, my career changed dramatically. I went from doing maybe 300 shoots a year for them, being out in the community on a regular basis to...maybe eight a year.

Donovan: Crazy!

Julie: That loss of history, through my eyes, is profound.

Donovan: That is profound.

Julie: The reporters were out doing it with their flip phones.

Donovan: Yeah, but that's different.

Julie: The archival storage alone is different. The loss of that history really worries me. But it flipped me from having this journalistic lens, this historical reporting and documentarian lens, to the more artistic. Now I was released. Just like you were doubted when you went to pursue—something I consider noble—a cause that ignited you as the artist you are. The quest I'm on now is all about a conversation and a visual record. But it is always collaborative. My work and your work really dovetails nicely.

Donovan: Yeah, and Emerson Street House is making that happen even more right now.

This audio recording has been edited and condensed for publication.

Document of a Dynamic Community: The Skanner Photography of Julie Keefe

- A Retrospective from 1987 to 2008 at the Oregon Historical Society

"Julie Keefe's Photos Show Beauty and Heartbreak of Northeast Portland."

- Aaron Scott, OBP (Oregon Public Broadcasting). November 25, 2016

https://www.opb.org/artsandlife/article/skanner-julie-keefe-photography-oregon-historical-society/

Nicole Sandoval standing in front of a Julie Keefe panel

"I am deeply grateful to Diane for creating and offering a safe space for meaningful connections and authentic relationships - A place for growth, as individuals and as a community, where everyone is welcomed and we can all belong. Emerson Street House is a glympse of what I wish Portland would become."

- Laura Lo Forti, Story Midwife, Vanport Mosaic

Acknowledgments

In Gratitude

To Nicole Sandoval aka Nikki Brown Clown, for her dedication to provide culturally specific books for all children and promoting home schooling.

To Guillermo Sandoval, Community Banker, for supporting his wife Nikki Brown Clown and the local Community through his work at Tri-County and Umpqua Banks. Special recognition to Guillermo and Nikki for their work with the children and teachers displaced by the Camp Fire in Paradise California

To Julie Keefe, for documenting life in Northeast Portland from 1987 to 2008. Special recognition for allowing the retrospective of Northeast Portland to be shown at The Emerson Street House

To The Skanner, for preserving history of Northeast Portland.

A Realtor's Tour of the Emerson Street House

Introduction

I purchased the property at 1006 NE Emerson Street from a goat farmer who needed the equity out of her rental property so she could build a new barn for her goats. I learned that the house on the property was built without permits and attention to building codes, a common practice in Northeast Portland, Oregon in the day. I attempted to remodel the house first. When it became evident that a remodel was not viable, I dreamed of a new vision.

My father had a stroke eight months before he passed, from which he never fully recovered. Dr. Roy Cacciaguida, my parents' doctor for many years, told me to find an Assisted Living / Skilled Nursing Facility. Neither parent had handled my father's stroke appropriately and they could not continue to live alone.

My father planned for my mother and himself to Age at Home. He purchased a condo in an over 55 community ten years before he was ready to sell their single-family home and move in. He served on the Condominium Association Board so he could assure the community was well-managed and well-maintained. He always envisioned himself as the caregiver for my mother. He never imagined he would become incapacitated by a stroke and unable to care for himself or my mother.

My parents moved to Brighton Gardens by Marriott in West Palm Beach. The year was 1997; the building was new, the staff was caring and professional, and the residents were happy and social. The problem: it wasn't profitable so cost cutting over time took its toll and eventually Marriott sold Brighton Gardens.

On my birthday, September 15, 2017, an article in the Palm Beach Post caught my eye, "We Averted a Catastrophe: Seniors Wilted at West Palm Home Post-Irma."

Oh my God, that is where my parents lived until their passing. Thanks to the West Palm Beach police and fire, all residents survived. What is deeply distressing is the lack of empathy and caring demonstrated by the management. Brighton Gardens had gone from a shiny new model, designed to provide quality end of life care to a place to warehouse the old and infirm in just 20 years.

Bricks and mortar can be beautiful and environmentally sustainable as built. But then what? Who lives there or works there or plays there? How is the experience for these folks? Do these buildings solve problems like homelessness, displacement, gentrification, affordable housing, healthcare? Or do these buildings create new problems?

Armed with my new MBA in Sustainable Systems from Bainbridge Graduate School (BGI) and cash from my recently liquidated Wall Street investments, I decided to invest My Own Money (MOM) to answer some of these questions.

Living Building Challenge

Jason F. McLennan taught the Certificate Program in Green Building at Bainbridge Graduate Institute, the second year of BGI's MBA Program in Sustainable Systems. Those were heady times for Green Building in Seattle, Washington.

Jason was consulting on the Bullitt Center, a commercial office building at the intersection of the Central District neighborhood, and Capitol Hill, Seattle, Washington. It was officially opened on Earth Day, April 22, 2013. The Bullitt Center was designed to be the greenest commercial building in the world, and was certified as a "Living Building" by the International Living Future Institute—which was founded by Jason F. McLennan.

On the bullittcenter.org web site, the Bullitt Center declares that the lifespan of building is 250 years. Yet less than ten years later, everything had changed. Work / Live / Eat / Play / Pray has become a reality for most families. The Big Tech Five (Amazon, Apple, Facebook, Google, Microsoft) all have built huge office complexes to accommodate their huge staffs. But employees came to love remote work first thrust upon them by the pandemic.

The "Living Building" certification by the International Living Future Institute is a point in time, yet a Living Building must constantly adapt to changes in the world around it in order to actually be a Living Building.

The Emerson Street House was conceived as a Passive Net Zero house. The concept appealed to me, but I really didn't totally comprehend what that meant. I thought the Original Design Build Team (ODBT) understood my vision but I soon learned they were more adept at gaslighting that construction. They were taking the little old lady with the money (me) for a long expensive ride. From this point forward I will refer to the ODBT since they have resigned from the Living Building Challenge.

Living Community Challenge

The Living Community Challenge is an extension of the Living Building Challenge. The Emerson Street House was built to accommodate many different community meetings. Both in the back usually referred to as the Accessory Dwelling Unit (ADU) and the Main House which was conceived as the main community space as long as I lived there.

Murthy Srinivas, BGI Classmate, convinced me to sign up for the Living Building / Living Community Challenge. Murthy was mentoring Marisa Zylkowski, a brilliant young woman, who epitomized the vision for the Living Building / Living Community Challenge. Marisa left the International Living Future Institute, shortly after we met at The Emerson Street House. Marisa assured me that her ILFI colleagues would provide the support I needed.

The Accessory Dwelling Unit (ADU)

Our Team learned quite after the fact that only skinny houses were allowed on the lot at 1006 NE Emerson Street so The Emerson Street House is considered a single-family home with five bedrooms and three baths. But I digress, this is our team's vision of the Emerson Street House.

The ADU was built for me to Age at Home. I have Charcot-Marie-Tooth, a disease that I was born with, inherited from my mother. My feet were increasingly painful and I need surgery to alleviate the pain. Dr. Elliott Michael DPM, Broadway Foot and Ankle, and I were discussing the procedure and the need for six to eight weeks bed rest with my foot elevated.

The ADU Kitchen

The ADU Kitchen was designed, according to Christopher Alexander, as a space that could change over time, accommodating a small family, teenage children, or elders. At the time, I lived alone and would not have any live-in help after my surgery. Neighbors would bring groceries, I could cook, do laundry, etc., by myself.

Out team chose IKEA Business Portland for the kitchen. IKEA seems to have gone downhill since then, perhaps because of the material shortages caused by the pandemic, a real shame since IKEA worked so well at The Emerson Street House.

The interior wall of the ADU is the kitchen. The cost was 20% of the cost of traditional cabinets and provided four times the storage.

First the panorama view of the great room, living room, dining room, kitchen, laundry, office, community meeting room…

Next IKEA drawers and storage…

The ADU Master Bedroom

Next, my bedroom, well hidden behind the privacy wall and next to the bathroom. I share my bedroom with Daphne, my grand dog, and family photos. My neighbor, Joanne Suell Green, gifted me the quilt on my bed, it is 300 years old and quilted by hand. The small quilt over my bed was quilted by Joanne Suell Green (Joanne's Quilts).

The Other ADU Bedroom

Whoops! It's missing. I think we were hiding the junk in there so Jen Sotolongo could get the good happy pictures for the realtor's tour.

The ADU Bathroom

The bathroom next to my bedroom—not handicap accessible, but the best we could do in a small space.

"Love Mother Earth". Mini-mural created by Sharon Koskoff, the Duchess of Deco, for my birthday gift.

The ADU Backyard Garden

Backyard garden as seen from the back of the great room. Great in the summer, not so great in the rainy season and the snow.

The ADU Accessible Entrance

The accessible entrance to the ADU, with my signature quote "I'm Done with This Conservation." Sign created by Wynde Dyer, Multi-Media Artist and Master Quilter.

The Main House

View of the Emerson Street House from the Street

"Everyone Belongs," the motto of the Emerson Street House. Sign created by Wynde Dyer, Tarp Quilt and Eclectic Artist.

"A Book Is A Dream You Can Hold in Your Hand," Neil Gaiman.

The Main House Entrance

is at the top of the accessible staircase and to the right, abutting the ADU window. Wynde Dyer's Tarp Quilts accent the cedar plank exterior.

Emerson House Mail Box

Complete with live roof garden and solar panels which light the windows, designed and installed by Emily Wobb, Portland Artist.

The Main House Roof Garden

The Main House Roof Garden is up the stairs and to the right. We will fly right up and out the door, leaving the inside until last. These photos were taken just after the City Repair event at the Emerson Street House, while their nest was still partially up.

The Main House Staircase

The Main House Kitchen and Laundry Room

IKEA kitchen and laundry room under the staircase

Moroccan tea service by Ovations Coffee Shop in the Pearl District

The Main House Great Room

Sitting area for Bonnie Meltzer
(very mixed media) Exhibit on Making Electricity

 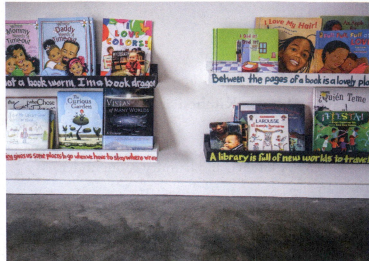

The Main House Downstairs Bedroom

The Main
House Downstairs
Bathroom

The Main House Upstairs Apartment

The upstairs apartment includes two bedrooms, a bath, and a private sitting area.

Upstairs sitting area, with a fold out couch for guests.

The Other Upstairs Apartment Bedroom

The room has two twin beds and a closet with a children's play area on the floor between the beds. Once again too messy for Jen Sotolongo, Photographer, to get good shots.

International Passive House Conference, Munich Germany 2018

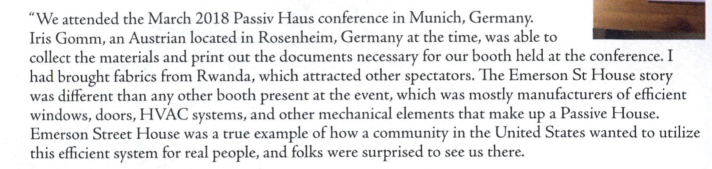

Mia Sheperd, Project Manager, for the Emerson Street House, flew off to Rwanda for an internship in building energy efficient low income housing. Mia received a notice about the Passive House Conference in Munich Germany, 9-10 March 2018.

Mia arranged for a hiatus from her internship, enlisted the help of Iris Gomm, her college classmate currently interning in Germany, bought a plane ticket and was good to go.

This is Mia's story in her own words..

"We attended the March 2018 Passiv Haus conference in Munich, Germany. Iris Gomm, an Austrian located in Rosenheim, Germany at the time, was able to collect the materials and print out the documents necessary for our booth held at the conference. I had brought fabrics from Rwanda, which attracted other spectators. The Emerson St House story was different than any other booth present at the event, which was mostly manufacturers of efficient windows, doors, HVAC systems, and other mechanical elements that make up a Passive House. Emerson Street House was a true example of how a community in the United States wanted to utilize this efficient system for real people, and folks were surprised to see us there.

We came to Munich with questions regarding the usability and functionality of the mechanical systems, which tested many of the engineers and technicians that came to chat with us. The answers were always similar, "don't touch the system." The Passive House goal is to build a completely sealed box, with the best air circulating, dehumidifying, heating, and cooling systems so you can live in the best environment that also reduces energy usage and in turn, helps the external environment. This system works best when you set it and walk away, which is a learning curve for those used to constantly adjusting the thermostat in their home, or opening and closing windows for fresh air.

Building a Passive House in conjunction with the Living Building Challenge is a way to make a space self-sufficient, and comfortable and use less energy on a day-to-day basis. Although this is not achievable for every home, it's what makes the Emerson St House an extremely special and architecturally iconic place in North East Portland. We were thrilled to share the story of how the Passive House standard made its way to Portland, OR, and learn from those in Germany about how their systems work best."

Building a Living Building and a Living Community

Most large conferences follow the same format as the Passiv Haus Conference. The technicians talk to each other, pat them selves on the back for the great work they are doing, and ignore the folks who have to use their products.

As an example, the HRV and water systems at the Emerson Street House were installed incorrectly by the ODBT. I never touched the system as instructed; instead I purchased portable thermostats from Amazon. These thermostats showed 10 degrees difference from the system thermostats. And the water system freezes up, causing ice to form which shuts down the hot water. I don't want to bore you with the litany of problems, but there were many more.

In my opinion, the bones and systems of an affordable home need to be functional and easy to maintain.

MLK Jr. Membership Model

Introduction

Dr Martin Luther King Jr. was a businessman before he was a pastor. I have often thought the "not-for-profit" world would be different if Dr. King had lived to a ripe old age. Turns out Uhura of the Starship Enterprise was Dr. King's surrogate as we learn from Wikipedia's entry on Nyota Uhura:

> "[Nichelle] Nichols planned to leave Star Trek in 1967 after its first season, wanting to return to musical theater. She changed her mind after talking to Martin Luther King Jr. who was a fan of the show. King explained that her character signified a future of greater racial harmony and cooperation. King told Nichols, "You are our image of where we're going, you're 300 years from now, and that means that's where we are and it takes place now. Keep doing what you're doing, you are our inspiration." As Nichols recounted, "Star Trek was one of the only shows that [King] and his wife Coretta would allow their little children to watch. And I thanked him and I told him I was leaving the show. All the smile came off his face. And he said, 'Don't you understand for the first time we're seen as we should be seen. **You don't have a Black role. You have an equal role.**'"

It turns out Uhura was also the role model for Nicole Sandoval aka Nikki Brown Clown:

> "Seeing [Uhura] on TV back when I was a little Black Girl growing up during a time when representation was still rare meant a lot to me. Especially because I was into sci-fi which filled those spaces are still barely filled with a Black Actress. She gave me hope that a Black girl like me can dream big, and live out her biggest fantasies! I even named my second child after Ms. Nichelle. This same child has a tattoo portrait of Ms. Nichols on their arm."

Work/ Live/ Eat/Play/ Pray

The pandemic lockdowns taught us that our homes must accommodate Work/ Live/ Eat/ Play/ Pray. We all had to do that for two weeks, which turned into two years plus. Finally some folks are challenging Fauci, the FDA, the CDC, our elected officials and other Federal agencies for plunging the robust US economy into recession.

The Emerson Street House was built using Alexander's *A Pattern Language* and Jacob's *"Eyes on the Street."*

Nicole and Guillermo Sandoval and family, the current owners and residents of the Emerson Street House are well prepared for the Work/ Live/ Eat/ Play/ Pray environment.

Dr. King knew that any business can be NONPROFIT. They just have to spend more than they bring in. A business can't do this for long before they go out of business and any GOOD they may have done goes down the drain.

CASH REVENUE IN < CASH REVENUE OUT = NONPROFIT

CASH REVENUE IN > CASH REVENUE OUT = HEALTHY BUSINESS MODEL

Dr. King's model is a Multiple Member LLC, which will be taxed as a Partnership. Attorneys and Accountants often use this model to manage their business. You know they have figured out thousands of ways to skin a cat, mostly so the head honchos can bring home the biggest paycheck. I am guessing we just need to flip the Attorney/ Accountant Model on its head to accomplish social justice and equity, which is my goal.

Executive Staff

Commander Nikki Brown Clown aka "Nikki" Sandoval and Assistant Commander Guillermo "Papi" Sandoval

Executive Staff In Training (SIT)

o Foster-to-Adopt Boy 1   o Foster-to-Adopt Boy 2   o Foster-to-Adopt Boy 3   o New Granddaughter

Operating Rules and Regulations

Commander "Nikki" and Assistant Commander "Papi" own the Emerson Street House, purchased on a 30 year, 3% , no down payment mortgage from the Emerson Street House LLC (Diane M Freaney, single-member LLC). No additional sponsorship funds are required since the Sandovals are already making monthly mortgage payments on the property.

The Sandovals are allowed to use all spaces inside and outside the property at 1006 NE Emerson Street,

Portland, OR 97211 as Live/ Work/ Eat/ Play/ Pray spaces in keeping with the tradition of Jane Jacobs and Christopher Alexander, et al.

The Sandovals are responsible for the maintenance and repair of the property, inside and outside, and may use funds raised by the MLK Jr. Membership Drive to keep the property immaculate and up-to-date in the tradition of International Net-Zero Passive Building Construction.

Emerson Street House Transitions

The Sandovals are responsible for providing a smooth transition when their time at the Command Center Emerson Street House comes to an end. Ideally the Executive Staff In Training (SIT) will be well-trained and one or more SITs will be ready to move into leadership roles.

My hope is that direct dependents of the current Sandoval family will assume leadership roles as long as Mother Earth exits. In the unlikely event that does not happen, my hope is that a local community-based organization will step forward to provide ongoing leadership.

MLK Jr. Marketing Model

The model I researched and designed for a historic church in Stuart is only the marketing component. Other components which are equally important, include legal, accounting, finance, taxation, location (state, county, municipality, rural), history, audience, etc.

The State of Florida, where I live now, is a little like the Wild West. I just finished reading **Not My First Rodeo: Lessons from the Heartland** by Kristi Noem, current governor of South Dakota. Kristi began ranching as soon as she was able to walk. I realized that the Florida that I love is more like South Dakota than the State of Oregon which I write about in the **What Is This Place?** book series.

Small businesses are the backbone of our economy. These are the businesses that the Emerson Street Community wants to become part of the Family.

The Emerson Street House is Sold

NEW HOMEOWNERS
September 22, 2022 with Guillermo Sandoval in Portland, Oregon

Dreams do come true!

I can't believe when we met 6 tears ago I lived 3 blocks away on this same NE Portland Street in an affordable housing building. I'd walk by this beautiful house as it was being build on my way to get my morning coffee and I often wondered who would be living in this beautiful modern home.

Thanks to my neighbors I'd soon meet the owner of this very home at the coffee shop and together we developed a unique friendship that led to us hosting several community block parties, art shows, concerts, a mural and lending library dedicated to my work as Nikki Brown Clown.

I have always been a key holding guest in this home but today with the help of my friend Diane and husband this is now my forever home!

EMERSON STREET COMMUNITY, A NEIGHORHOOD CO-OPERATIVE

This project explores how the Living Community Challenge can be used as a tool by existing residential neighborhoods to not only maximize the social and environmental benefits of community redevelopment, but also address some of the inherent challenges: maintaining affordability for existing residents, guarding against gentrification, and minimizing the displacement of homes, businesses, and institutions. The site is the Emerson Street Community, an 80-acre section of dense residential development in Northeast Portland's former, historically African-American, Albina neighborhood, with one of the most racially, culturally, and socio-economically diverse populations in the city. The project team – includes all community residents, community-based artists, Oregon Benefits Companies, local non-profits and allied professionals — sees synergies in promoting energy efficiency, building resilient infrastructure, and activating resident owners and tenants to strengthening neighborhood relationships and create a restorative and sustainable live-work community.

—Introduction by Nicholas Papaefthimiou

Emerson Street Community,
80-acre Section of Dense Residential Development

Nicholas printed some pages from Portland Maps and sketched out the 80-acre section of dense residential development. We spent an hour identifying key people and places in and adjacent to the 80-acre, all within walking distance.

near King — Por
NE Grand Ave
NE 6th Ave
NE 7th Ave
NE 8th Ave
NE 9th Ave
NE Ainsworth St
NE Simpson St
NE 10th Ave
NE 11th Ave
NE 12th Ave
NE 13th Ave
NE Jarrett St
NE Jarrett St
NE Jarrett St
NE 7th Ave
NE Jessup St
NE 9th Ave
NE Church St
NE Church St
NE Killingsworth St
NE 6th Ave
NE 12th Ave
NE 13th Ave
Emerson St
NE Emerson St
Roselawn St
NE Roselawn St
NE Sumner St
NE Sumner St
NE Webster St
NE Webster St
NE 6th Ave
NE Alberta St
NE Grand Ave
NE 7th Ave
NE 8th Ave
500
1,000 feet

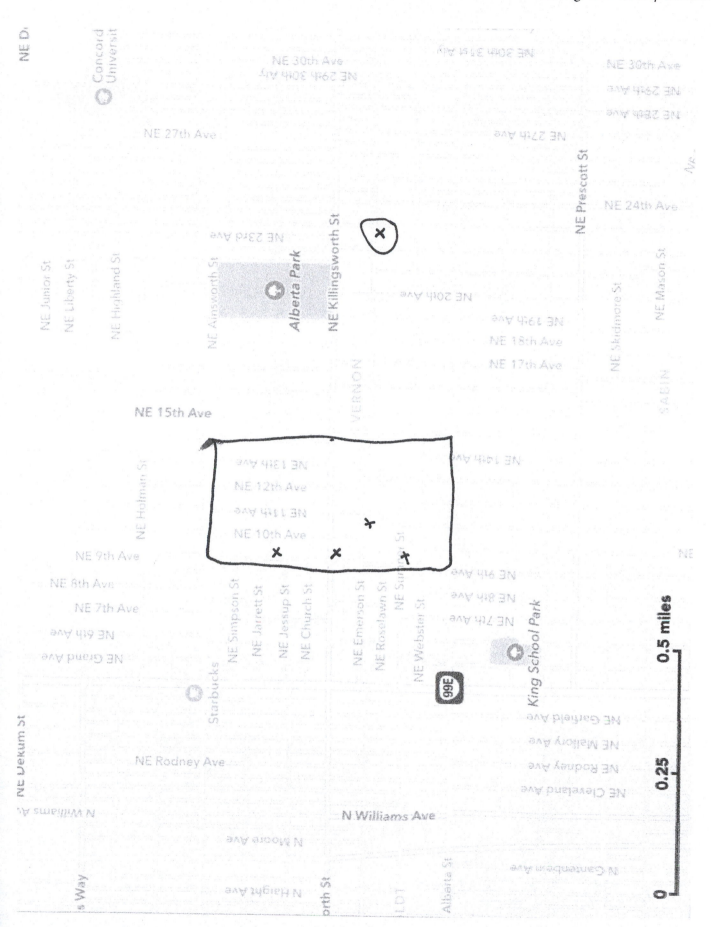

Historic Black Churches:
Models for Living Communities

As we competed with other projects to become the first Registered Project to complete the Living Community Challenge, one thing became clear. The Emerson Street Community is the only project which has people on it's landing page, a racially, culturally and socio-economically diverse group of folks.

Beautiful buildings, grounds and expensive public art are nice, but do they provide the sustenance that ordinary folks need to live a healthy and happy life?

As I pondered this questions, I was drawn to religious institutions, as they seemed to have the caring and camaraderie that I craved. I moved back to Florida and my quest continued. I gravitated toward two churches, both with powerful woman at the helm, and began my research to understand their process in building Living Communities.

St. Monica's Episcopal Church, Stuart Florida, established 1928

The history of St. Monica's Episcopal Church...

"St. Monica's historic journey began as a basic worship gathering in the Home of Willie and Alice Christie in Stuart, Martin County in 1924. St. Monica's was the first Black church with a European style of service; chartered by the City in 1928.

St. Monica's original Parish Hall was the first and only Church venue in the community for African American social and civic gatherings for a long time. St. Monica's was a major meeting place for many important community initiatives, related to Desegregation, and the Civil Rights movement."

Senior Warden Eula Clark and Rev. Donna Small, Priest

Eula R. Robinsin-Clarke is an Immigrant

Eula Robinson was 18 when she moved with her family from Jamaica to Belle Glade. Miss Robinson studied and worked hard; an MS in urban and regional planning in 1981; a law degree in 1996 and was elected to the City of Stuart Commission in 2011. She is married to Dennis Clarke, a Local 728 master electrician, and they have two sons - Hugh and Chad.

Eula Clarke's Motto

"No man is an island, no man stands alone; each man's joy is joy to me, each man's grief is my own, We need one another, so I will defend each man as my brother, each man as my friend." — Joan Baez. No Man is An Island

165

St. Monica's Needs an Infusion of Youth

St. Monica's story is the story of many religious institutions today. COVID forced most churches to Zoom or stop regular services altogether. Church members drifted away, physically and spiritually.

From its founding in 1924 until sometime in the eighties, St. Monica's was the community center for Black folks in Stuart, Martin County. Young Black folks followed a different path, mostly a positive path as the trades and other good paying jobs opened up for them, allowing them to buy homes, start families, travel, pursue hobbies and other activities that may have taken the place of worship when they had free time.

At the same time, many not-for profit organizations that fulfill community needs formerly filled by religious organizations, came into being. These organizations are inclusive by design, often serving the entire family, just as St. Monica's did in the past.

Active and Passive Community Members

Broadly speaking, all humans are either active or passive most of the time. Eula Clarke is very passionate, always pushing to reach the next level of achievement to help herself, her family, her community, her church and all her fellow human beings.

Her passion has lead others to pilot more community building projects.

> **"The way to a man's heart is through his stomach."**
> **—Fanny Fern, July 9, 1811 - October 10, 1872)**

Saint Monica's Episcopal Church Cookbook (1998)

All church members will rise to the occasion for a project that strikes their fancy. At a Coffee Klatch after church Sunday, several congregants shared their stories over ginger beer and pastries. The idea of updating the Cookbook printed for a fund-raiser in 1998 surfaced. Twenty-five years later so many things have changed.

Helen Christie

The church ladies were talking about medicinal cures common in the Bahamas, how to make the Bahamian teas, St. Monica's Famous Friday night Fish Fry and Saturday morning breakfasts for the local community members.

Check out the 2023 version of *St. Monica's Episcopal Church Cookbook*, promoting health and happiness in East Stuart Florida.

New Hope Missionary Baptist Church, Lake Worth Beach Florida, established 1940

History of New Hope Missionary Baptist Church...

"Pastor Ira A. Banks started New Hope Missionary Baptist Church, which served the Historic Lake Osborne District for 35 years (1940-1975). Sunday services were held on Sister Mandy Marshall's front porch until the church had enough members and money to build a proper community church.

Pastor W. H. Hardemon (1978-2007) installed stained glass windows and lighting in the sanctuary and added Hardemon Hall, a community center used for socializing after church, meals after weddings, birthdays, and other community meetings. Pastor Hardemon was the voice of the community, respected by national, state and local officials.

Pastor Cato and Sister Lowe

In 2008, Pastor/Teacher Tony L. Cato was called to serve New Hope Missionary Baptist Church. New Hope became a "a lighthouse for those saved and desiring to be save!" Pastor Cato challenges church members to "Embrace a Spirit of Excellence" and "To Give God Our Best."

Retha Mae Lowe, 50-year Resident, Lake Worth

Retha Mae moved to her current home in "the District, "Lake Worth as the new bride of Grady Lowe, Jr. "When I moved here 50 years ago, we were separated. We didn't deal with downtown, we didn't deal with the whites, we stayed in our own little area."

Retha ventured out of "the District" to study at Palm Beach Junior College and embark on a career as a banker, starting out as a teller, progressing to service representative and branch manager at a bank in downtown Lake Worth (1972-1994). In addition, Retha was in charge of the Lowe household and raising the four Lowe children, three sons and a daughter.

Retha and Grady had a good marriage until Grady's passing on July 4, 2020.

New Hope Missionary Baptist Church is a Business

Retha invited me to meet Pastor Cato after Sunday Service. Pastor Cato and the New Hope Leadership Team know that church is a business, and 501 (c) (3) organizations are a section of the Internal Revenue Code. New Hope only added a 501 (c) (3) in 2016 to satisfy the requirement for a local government grant.

Even the name selected for the 501(c)(3) organizations reflects New Hope's philosophy -

HOPE MINISTRIES COMMUNITY DEVELOPMENT, INC.

Rooted Investing

THE ART AND SCIENCE OF INVESTING FLEW OUT THE WINDOW IN 2023.

My financial net worth would be six or seven times what it is now if I had not sold all my Wall Street investments in 2013 and continued my conservative investing style. And yet that would have left me morally bankrupt.

Even as the bad actors like Sam Bankman-Fried and others of his ilk has found new ways to scam customers, GOOD emerges in the financial sector. These are a few examples…

Nicholas Papaefthimiou| infillPDX

Nicholas founded infillPDX, LLC in 2014 to showcase the affordable housing models units owned and operated by his family. Nick is a hands on Design Build, General Contractor and Landlord. Nick understands architecture and engineering theory perfectly, but always has to test the theory out for himself.

I was privileged to finance three infillPDX projects. These projects were my best Rooted Investing investments.

Nick was already highly skilled at design build and general contracting, but he had a lot to learn about being a landlord. He patiently worked with his tenants who needed to learn to be good neighbors as well as good tenants. Nick learned as his tenants learned and used his new learning to tackle larger, more complex affordable housing projects, using sustainable building techniques.

Affordable housing is often shoddily built because developer starts with the glossy images of a high end development and just use cheaper materials and equipment and a "one size fits all" kind of approach. Before long the flaws start to show and the tenants suffer with broken appliances, leaks and lack of privacy from paper thin walls.

Guillermo Sandoval, Financial Inclusion Director, Umpqua Bank

Guillermo has spent most of his career working in affordable housing and community development, mostly for Pacific Northwest Banks. The closing on the Emerson Street House was so easy. Guillermo's colleagues in community development volunteered legal services, which kept closing costs to a minimum. The agenct for the title company had never seen a no money down mortgage before and Guillermo had to keep reassuring her that this was not a typo.

Past bankers in my life were almost always good bankers like Guillermo. That changed as Quicken Mortgage became dominant in the field. I hope that changes as our lawmaker start to unravel the economic chaos of 2023.

Javier, Branch Leader, TRUIST Bank

A friend who is on permanent medical disability manages her meager funds well. Recently she took out a branded credit card, with a well-known appliance store that is also a known scammer.
She missed a payment date by two days when she was training for a new part-time job. This triggered a demand for increased payments which would have eaten up her entire social security check.

Javier saw her distress when she arrived at TRUIST to deposit the check from her part-time job. He helped her payoff the offending credit card, replaced with a TRUIST credit card for emergencies. He gave her budgeting tips appropriate for her income level and promised to watch her account.

Connect Credit Union and Flagler Bank

My banks are Connect Credit Union, personal, and Flagler Bank, commercial. I opened an account at Connect Credit Union when I first moved to Stuart Florida. My new businesses - Emerson House Press and Emerson House Art Gallery - were different from my Freaney & Company LLC which only provided bookkeeping and accounting services, reported by clients on Form 1099 for income tax purposes.

My first royalties for Emerson House Press were direct deposited to my personal account - and immediately returned to the sender. Why I asked? "You need to have a commercial account for royalty payments," said my member services representative.

I redirected the direct deposit of royalties to my account at Flagler Bank, a regional commercial bank. Both Connect Credit Union and Flagler Bank have excellent customer service representatives who are familiar with their customers. I have credit cards with both and will automatically receive a "fraud alert" when unusual transactions occur in my accounts.

Rooted Investing

https://www.dianefreaney.com/rooted-investing

+ Emerson Street Community
+ Emerson Street House
+ Duncan Farms Oregon
+ Nicholas Papaefthimiou
+ Taylor Lucas Mortgage
+ Dave Hoch Student Loan
+ Duschka Fowler-Dunning Student Loan
+ Aaron Barnes | The 1905 Music Venue
+ Michelle DePass Automobile Loan

Photograph of Nicole Sandoval courtesy of Julie Keefe

Cultural Activities in the Emerson Street Community

Portland to Lake Worth Art Drive 2019
https://www.dianefreaney.com/art-drive-from-portland

Community Walking Tours
https://www.dianefreaney.com/emerson-street-community-walking-tours

- Sharon Koskoff in Portland Oregon
- 13th Avenue Walking Tour
- Alberta Street Nighttime Walking Tour
- Alberta Street Daytime Walking Tour
- 42nd Avenue Walking Tour
- New Seasons (3445 North Williams Street)
- Art Deco NE PDX

Community Activities
https://www.dianefreaney.com/community-activities

- Design Week Portland 2017
- Leave No Trace
- Diane's Birthday September 15, 2016
- Kudos and Criticism

Past Exhibitors at the Emerson Street House
https://www.dianefreaney.com/exhibitors-at-emerson-street-house

- Patrick Zahn | Steel Door Gallery
- Robin Corbo | Muralist, Artist, Educator
- Julie Keefe | Community-Based, Fine Artist
- The Art of Jimmy Tsutomu Mirikitani
- Carl Conrad | Portland Artist

Mr. Bobby
https://www.dianefreaney.com/mr-bobby-fouther

- Mr. Bobby
- Liz Fouther-Branch

Woodstove House Parties Series

https://www.dianefreaney.com/woodstove-music-house-parties

- Ky Burt | Creator, Host, and Curator | Woodstove House Parties Series
- Ky Burt | The Sky in Between
- Ky Burt | Duncan Farms Oregon
- Clara Baker
- March to May
- Heather Monahan
- Grace Love
- Nadine's Soul Kitchen
- Run boy Run Band
- The Absentees
- Max's Midnight Kitchen
- Hollis Peach
- Joel Shupack
- Matt Meighan Artichoke Music
- Magda Leyna

ACKNOWLEDGMENTS

REAL PEOPLE

Professionals who Volunteered their Time and Expertise to Complete the Living Building Challenge / Living Community Challenge

My mind is boggled as I think of all the people who have blessed the Emerson Street House. Some folks prefer to remain anonymous, which I want to respect. If you are not on the list, I have decided that you are among the many folks who like to work quietly in the background.

Felecia Hatcher and Derick Pearson, Black Tech Week, Miami
Kadi McLean, McLean Brand Development (Marketing Maven)
Nicholas Papaefthimiou, AIA, LEED BD+C, Architect and Structural Engineer, MIT, UC Berkeley, Investor and Developer of Affordable Housing, Founder Infill PDX
Cory Huff, The Abundant Artist
Muffie Delgado Connelly, Dancer
Robin Corbo, Muralist
Mark Lakeman, Grassroots Urban Placemaking
Kirk Rhea, City Repair
Mia Sheperd, Cal Poly (Architecture and Environmental Design)
Iris Gomm, Cal Poly (Architecture and Environmental Design)
Ky Burt, Singer/ Songwriter and Music Therapist
Tommy Blockson, Dog Walker Extraordinaire and Emerson Street neighbor
Kevin Beasley, Multimedia Journalist, University of Oregon, Navy Veteran
Zach Putnam, ZPproductions, Filmmaker, Producer, Head Cheerleader
Joanne Suell Green, Emerson Street neighbor and Joanne's Quilts
Vanessa White, Emerson Street neighbor, entrepreneur, and model parent, grandparent, and homeowner.
S. Renee Mitchell, Renaissance Woman and Teacher Extraordinaire

ACTIVISTS AND VISIONARIES

Christopher Alexander - From his Amazon Author's Page

Alexander's most important work is *A Pattern Language: Towns, Buildings, Construction and The Timeless Way of Building.*

Alexander was born in Vienna, Austria and raised in Oxford and Chichester, England. He was awarded the top open scholarship to Trinity College, Cambridge in 1954, in chemistry and physics, and went on to read mathematics at Cambridge. He took his doctorate in architecture at Harvard (the first Ph.D. in architecture ever awarded at Harvard), and was elected to the society of Fellows at Harvard University in 1961. During the same period, he worked at MIT in transportation theory and in computer science, and at Harvard in cognitive science. His pioneering ideas from that time were known to be highly influential in those fields.

Alexander became Professor of Architecture at the University of California, Berkeley in 1963, and taught there continuously for 38 years, becoming Professor Emeritus in 2001. He founded the Center for Environmental Structure in 1967, published hundreds of papers and several dozen books, and built more than 200 buildings around the world.

Alexander is widely recognized as the father of the pattern language movement in computer science, which has led to important innovations such as Wiki, and new kinds of Object-Oriented Programming.

Jane Jacobs - From her Amazon Author's Page

Thirty years after its publication, *The Death and Life of Great American Cities* was described by the New York Times as "perhaps the most influential single work in the history of town planning.... [It] can also be seen in a much larger context. It is, first, a work of literature; the descriptions of street life as a kind of ballet and the bitingly satiric account of traditional planning theory can still be read for pleasure even by those who long ago absorbed and appropriated the book's arguments."

Jane Jacobs, an editor and writer on architecture in New York City in the early sixties, argued that urban diversity and vitality were being destroyed by powerful architects and city planners. Rigorous, sane, and delightfully epigrammatic, Jacobs's small masterpiece is a blueprint for the humanistic management of cities. It is sensible, knowledgeable, readable, indispensable.

From one regret is that Jane Jacobs and I did not meet in person. I lived in New York City around the time Jane Jacobs was living in Greenwich Village and battling Robert Moses. I was busy being good little girl accountant and did not understand the gravity of her work at the time.

Cara Brookins - From her Amazon Author's Page

"Cara Brookins is professional speaker based in Little Rock and is best known for being the mom who built her own house using YouTube tutorials. She has been entertaining, educating, and inspiring audiences with her keynotes and presentations since 2004. She is the author of eight books, including *Rise, How a House Built a Family*, which tells the story of building her 3500 square foot house with the help of her four children by watching YouTube tutorials and googling things like foundation work, plumbing, and gas lines. News of Cara's family story went viral in more than 65 countries and was viewed a billion times. Rise, has now been optioned to become a major motion picture. Inspiring audiences to build bigger lives remains her greatest passion."

Living Community Work
- Other Community Collaborations

The word today is multi-media, not just the printed word in the form of books, blogs and newsletters, but podcasts, videos, live streaming, websites, social media, and other media that translates poorly to the written word.

For the Living Community Challenge, we are focusing our energy on the four soft petals *Beauty, Equity, Health and Happiness, Place*. We are in negotiations with Martin Pearl Press, a traditional publisher with specialties in children's books and historical fiction, to move their headquarters from Dixon, California to Stuart, Florida.

Books

Freaney, Diane. *Complexity = Corruption: The US Tax System*. Emerson House Press. 2023.
_____ *Complexity = Corruption: The US Education System*. Emerson House Press. 2023
_____ *Complexity = Corruption: The US Healthcare System*. Emerson House Press. 2023
_____ *Complexity = Corruption: The US Mental Health System*. Emerson House Press. 2023
_____ *FAU and the Red Corvette Scandal*. Emerson House Press. 2023.
_____ *The Adventures of Stacy and Diane*. Emerson House Press. 2023.
_____ *The Art of Jimmy Tsutomu Mirikitani, A Traveling Exhibit of the Wing Luke Museum*. Emerson House Press. 2022.
_____ *What is This Place? A Realtor's Tour of the Emerson Street House*. Emerson House Press. 2022.
_____ *What is This Place? Conversations Around the Emerson Street House*. Emerson House Press. 2021.
_____ *What is This Place? MLK Jr. Membership Model*. Emerson House Press. 2022.
Honda, Loriene PhD. *The Cat Who Chose to Dream*. Martin Pearl Press. 2014.

Cookbooks

Autographed copies of these cookbooks are collector's items and will become more valuable over time. An investment in your health and nutrition is also a good financial investment. Or you can purchase a copy, without autograph, on Amazon.com.

New Hope Missionary Baptist Church Community Cookbook. Emerson House Press. 2023. To purchase a copy autographed by New Hope's cookbook committee, mail a check for $50.00 to New Hope Missionary Baptist Church, 819 Washington Avenue, Lake Worth Beach, FL 33460.

St. Monica's Episcopal Church Cookbook. Emerson House Press. 2023. To purchase a copy autographed by St. Monicas's cookbook committee, mail a check for $50.00 to PO Box 1798, Stuart FL 34995.

The Pelican Cookbook: Food Made With Love. Emerson House Press. 2023. To purchase a copy autographed by Tara, mail a check for $50.00 to The Pelican Cookbook, c/o aioli, 7434 S Dixie Highway, West Palm

Beach, FL 33405.

Podcasts

Tiny House Podcast # 139 We're Way Off the Reservation with Diane Freaney and the Emerson Street House. Michelle (MJ) Bredeson, Mark Grimes and Perry. Sound Cloud. April 7, 2018. https://on.soundcloud.com/umqhn

Videos

Filmed by ODBT (Original Design Build Team)

Freaney, Diane. *Rooted Investing: A Conversation with Diane Freaney.* 2013. https://vimeo.com/117611957

Freaney, Diane. *Rooted Investing: A Housing Model for a Better Future.* 2014. https://vimeo.com/117312673

Emerson Street House Meeting: Diane Freaney and two ODBT Members 10-3-2014. https://vimeo.com/479286224

Videos Shot by Drone by ODBT (Original Design Build Team)

ODBT's Photographer and Son 8-3-2015. https://vimeo.com/479345346
1006 NE Emerson Street - Concrete Pour 1. https://vimeo.com/479282238
1006 NE Emerson Street - Concrete Pour 2. https://vimeo.com/479283319
1006 NE Emerson Street - Concrete Pour 3. https://vimeo.com/479284894
ODBT's Drone Photo Preparing for Trusses 9-29-2015. https://vimeo.com/479342720
ODBT's Drone Shot of Lifting Trusses 9-29-2015. https://vimeo.com/479347666
ODBT's Landscape Architect Speaks on Benefits of a Green Roof. https://vimeo.com/246726118

EMC Charles Waylan Rogers, Retired Navy Seal, ("Chuck").

Chuck was my breakfast buddy at Aunt D's Diner in Stuart for the two years it was open. Chuck and I were both "early birds," arriving promptly at 6:30am. Chuck loved to talk about his service to his country, working in the jungles of Korea and Vietnam for "the man," aka the CIA.

I hired a local videographer to film Chuck's story at Aunt D's Diner and asked Chuck to wear his uniform, which he normally only does on Veteran's Day and Memorial Day. Local videographer did an amazing job, so good that his video attracted the slime balls that prey on honest folks on YouTube. Even Chuck's biological son joined in the sliming, alleging that Chuck was not a Navy Seal.

From Wikipedia: United States Navy SEALS…

> "**Although not formally founded until January 1, 1962, the modern-day U.S. Navy SEALs trace their roots to World War II.** The United States Military recognized the need for the covert reconnaissance of landing beaches and coastal defenses. As a result, the joint Army, Marine Corps, and Navy Amphibious Scout and Raider School was established in 1942 at Fort Pierce, Florida. The Scouts and Raiders were formed in September of that year, just nine months after the attack on Pearl Harbor, from the Observer Group, a joint U.S. Army-Marine-Navy unit."

> "The Central Intelligence Agency (CIA) began using SEALs in covert operations in early 1963. The SEALs

were later involved in the CIA sponsored Phoenix Program where it targeted Vietcong (VC) infrastructure and personnel for capture and assassination."

Life Legacy Stories of Chuck Rogers, Retired Navy SEAL. November 20, 2021. https://vimeo.com/663429420

One of Chuck's careers after retiring from the Navy was restoring/ renovating historic properties. Chuck agreed to review and comment on the ODBT's photos and videos of the construction of the Emerson Street House.

Construction of the Emerson Street House: Narrated by Chuck Rogers. Edited by Rick Miller, Treasure Coast Multimedia. https://vimeo.com/693554635

*Construction of the Emerson Street House: Narrated by Chuck Rogers (**WITH CAPTIONS**).* Edited by Rick Miller, Treasure Coast Multimedia. https://vimeo.com/809081258

Chuck documented his restorations/ renovations in videos. Some of these videos…

Restoration of Water Damage Elliston Vineyard, Sunol Valley, Alameda County, California. March 1990. Chuck Rogers. March 1990. https://vimeo.com/693560286

01 Chuck Remodel 1990. Chuck Rogers. 1990. https://vimeo.com/680567916

02 Chuck Remodel 1993. Chuck Rogers. 1993. https://vimeo.com/680570668

03 Chuck Remodel 1994. Chuck Rogers. 1994. https://vimeo.com/680572246

04 Chuck Remodel 1995. Chuck Rogers. 1995. https://vimeo.com/680574229

05 Chuck Remodel Two Story House. Chuck Rogers. https://vimeo.com/680575511

Other Living Community Videos.

Black Tech Week Founders. Felecia Hatcher and Derick Pearson, Diane Freaney, Emcee. June 2015. https://vimeo.com/manage/videos/811348132

Conversation Around Local Investing. Eli Spevak, Orange Splot LLC, Derick Pearson and Felecia Hatcher, Center for Black Innovation, S. Renee Mitchell, PhD, Creative Revolutionist, Diane Freaney, Emcee. June 2015. https://vimeo.com/manage/videos/811322653

Vision for the Emerson Street House: Narrated by Diane Freaney. Diane Freaney. 2018. https://vimeo.com/246722747

Tommie Walking Daphne on Emerson Street. Tommie Blockson. 2019. https://vimeo.com/479503203

The Living Community Challenge: Emerson Street House. Diane Freaney. Videography and Editing by Rick Miller, Treasure Coast Multimedia. April 9, 2021. https://vimeo.com/534967416

The Living Community Challenge: Raw Footage. Diane Freaney. Videography by Rick Miller, Treasure Coast Multimedia. April 9, 2021. https://vimeo.com/532347447

Duncan Farms

The Story of Duncan Farms in Gales Creek, Oregon: Narrated by Jeremy Jensen. Videography and Editing by Kevin Beasley. 2019. https://vimeo.com/288221996

The Highwaymen

"The Highwaymen" - Stuart Heritage Museum Monthly Community Program. https://youtu.be/RPYyeN8-WXY

Epilogue

One Door Closes...

My work on the Living Building / Living Community Challenge in Portland, Oregon is finished and I pass the torch to the folks you have met earlier in this book and their families, friends, and colleagues.

My biggest joy in completing the Living Community Challenge was in circling back and catching up with folks that I once worked with on a daily basis. I learned that their worlds are changing even faster than mine because they are younger and more agile. I had so many aha moments.

One paragraph might take me half a day to write as I dug deep into stories on websites, Facebook or Wikipedia. I used to think I needed to solve every problem I encountered. I learned that was not only impossible but crazy thinking.

Somehow Karma brings like-minded folks together, each working on a solution in their own way, for a final solution which is more life affirming than I could have imagined.

I close this chapter of my life in love and gratitude to the people who I met and for the experiences I had this past fourteen years, and I move on to the next chapter of my life.`

Another Door Opens...

My Florida life in the cities of Stuart and Lake Worth Beach have not been without challenges, often mired in controversy. Retha Mae Lowe says, "GOOD! Change happens when there is controversy." In our short conversation, Retha rattled off a list of problems in our communities, many caused by COVID-19.

I tell folks that I will resume writing political books now that the LBC / LCC project is complete. "What topics?" Folks usually ask. My answer...

Complexity = Corruption

- US Tax System

- US Mental Health System

- US Healthcare System

- US Education System

- US Affordable Housing System

- US Military System

- and on it goes.

Folks are most passionate about the failed US Mental Health System. My writing process is to do a deep dive into research, hopefully weeding out "fake news" and to include my own experience - the good, the bad and the ugly. I often rely on some experts with a long history in the field to help me understand the problem and develop recommended solutions.

Today it seems every person in the United States is an expert on the US Mental Health System; some because of education, professional skills and licenses; others because of COVID caused issues in the family, the community and community organizations; some for both.

Florida is a hotbed of controversy in 2023 so I expect many good changes this year and in years to come.

Michelle Bredeson Boyle

Admin · April 25, 2018 · 🌐

...

Some days it's good to put on a different hat, and have a different conversation...

#139 We're Way Off the Reservation with Diane Freaney and Emerson Street House

What is Emerson Street House? Well we never really found out because our interview with intrepid Diane Freeney, Wall Street banker turned community advocate, roamed so far from housing and tiny houses, even we lost our way. It was a great conversation nonetheless, ranging from praising President Donald Trump, lambasting the construction trade, solving education in the US, building communities, and most interestingly: how not to build a passive solar home. Join us for one of the wildest conversations we've had in a l-o-n-g time. Even we were surprised. It's a wild and woolly walkabout through what lights Diane's fire on this episode of Tiny House Podcast!

Resources

Books

Alexander, Christopher et al. *A Pattern Language: Towns, Buildings, Construction.* Oxford University Press (New York). 1977.

_____ *The Oregon Experiment.* Oxford University Press (New York). 1975.

_____ *The Timeless Way of Building.* Oxford University Press (New York). 1979.

Brookins, Cara. *Rise: How a House Built a Family.* St. Martin's Press (New York). 2017.

Ford, Jamie. *Hotel on the Corner of Bitter and Sweet.* Ballentine Books (New York). 2009.

Hatcher, Felecia. *How to Start a Business on a Ramen Noodle Budget.* Feverish Holdings. 2013.

_____ *The C Students Guide to Scholarships: A Creative Guide to finding Scholarships when your grades suck and your parents are broke.* Feverish Holdings. 2012.

_____ *Start Your Business on a Ramen Noodle Budget: 12 Lessons on Becoming a Young Entrepreneur When You are Broke!* Peterson's. 2016.

Howley, Josh. *The Tyranny of Big Tech.* Regency Publishing (Washington, DC). 2021.

International Passive House Conference 2018. 9-10 March 2018 Munich.

Jacobs, Jane. *The Death and Life of Great American Cities.* New York: Random House, 1961.

Mitchell, S. Renee. *The Awakening of Sharyn: A Shy & Brown Super Gyrl.* Nappy Roots Press. 2012.

_____ *I Dare You.* Nappy Roots Press. 2013.

_____ *Thought you knew: Poetic testimonies about life, liberation and love.* Nappy Roots Press. 2002.

_____ *Tangoing with Tornadoes: A Novel.* Nappy Roots Press. 2013.

Noem, Kristi, *Not My First Rodeo: Lessons from the Heartland.* Hachette Book Group (New York). 2022.

Reports and Studies

1992 Alberta Street Cultural Resource Inventory with Recommendations. Robert Zybach, PhD and Michael "Chappie" Grice, Urban Forestry, Inc. 1992.

Wikipedia

1948 Columbia River flood https://en.wikipedia.org/wiki/1948_Columbia_River_flood

Benefit corporation https://en.wikipedia.org/wiki/Benefit_corporation

Bullitt Foundation | Capitol Hill, Seattle Washington | Certified as a Living Building by the International Living Future Institute https://en.wikipedia.org/wiki/Bullitt_Center

Christopher Alexander | American/British | Trinity, Cambridge, Harvard, MIT https://en.wikipedia.org/wiki/Christopher_Alexander

Fanny Fern | The way to a man's heart is through his stomach. https://en.wikipedia.org/wiki/Fanny_Fern

Guion Bluford https://en.wikipedia.org/wiki/Guion_Bluford

Independent Community Bankers of America https://en.wikipedia.org/wiki/Independent_Community_Bankers_of_America

Jane Jacobs | American/ Canadian | Journalist, author, urban theorist https://en.wikipedia.org/wiki/Jane_Jacobs

Jason F. McLennan | Canadian | Born, Sudbury Ontario https://en.wikipedia.org/wiki/Jason_F._McLennan

Marisa Zylkowski (Hagney) Sustainability | Architecture | Design https://www.linkedin.com/in/marisazylkowski

Mark Grimes. https://www.linkedin.com/in/mark-grimes/

Martin Luther King, Jr. https://en.wikipedia.org/wiki/Martin_Luther_King_Jr.

Maxville, Oregon https://en.wikipedia.org/wiki/Maxville,_Oregon

Mean Girls. https://en.wikipedia.org/wiki/Mean_Girls

Nyota Uhura https://en.wikipedia.org/wiki/Nyota_Uhura

Olive or Twist https://en.wikipedia.org/wiki/Olive_or_Twist

Sally Ride https://en.wikipedia.org/wiki/Sally_Ride

There ain't no such thing as a free lunch https://en.wikipedia.org/wiki/There_ain't_no_such_thing_as_a_free_lunch

United States Navy SEALs. https://en.wikipedia.org/wiki/United_States_Navy_SEALs

Vanport, Oregon https://en.wikipedia.org/wiki/Vanport,_Oregon

Wallowa County, Oregon https://en.wikipedia.org/wiki/Wallowa_County,_Oregon

Websites

Center for Black Innovation https://www.cfbi.org

Children's Entertainment |Nikki Brown Clown https://www.nikkibrownclown.com

Felecia Hatcher https://www.feleciahatcher.com

Highwaymen Art Specialists Inc. |Roger Lightle. https://highwaymenartspecialists.com/about/

Maxville Heritage Interpretive Center https://www.maxvilleheritage.org

Mr. B (Bobby Fouther) https://www.facebook.com/bobbyfouther

New Hope Missionary Baptist Church http://www.new-hope-mbc.org

Orange Splot LLC https://www.orangesplot.net

Panama Hotel & Japanese American Museum of Seattle https://panamahotelseattle.com

Pitch Black PDX https://www.pitchblackpdx.com

PJCE (Portland Jazz Composers Ensemble) „From Maxville to Vanport" multimedia program http://pjce.org/maxville-to-vanport/; „From Maxville to Vanport" full album https://pjce.bandcamp.com/album/from-maxville-to-vanport

Renee Mitchell Speaks https://www.reneemitchellspeaks.com

St. Monica's Episcopal Church http://www.stmonicas.org

Williams College Class of 1966 Environmental Center https://env-center.williams.edu/a-living-building

Newspapers Articles

Brown, DeNeen L. *A look at Oregon's shameful history as an 'all-white' state.* Washington Post. June 17, 2017.

Dupuy, Donna. *St. Monica's welcomes new priest.* TCPalm. March 24, 2016.

Feuer, Alan. *The Bank Around the Corner.* New York Times. December 23, 2011.

Kline, Allissa. *Bank of Cattaraugus hires within for new CEO.* Buffalo Business First. March 19, 2019.

Page, Sydney. *Why this teacher keeps one chair empty in his classroom.* Washington Post. August 12, 2022

Rodrigue, Donald. *Black History Month movers and shakers.* Hometown News. February 3, 2022.

Smith, Donovan. *Revisiting Alberta: Proposed new look at issues comes with racial lens.* Portland Observer. June 25, 2014.

Multi-Media Journalism

Carbonare, Jossie. *'We stayed in our own little area': Former vice mayor reflects on what segregation was like in Lake Worth Beach.* 25 WPBF News. January 16, 2023.

YouTube Videos

Lightly, Roger. *"The Highwaymen."* Stuart Heritage Museum. February 13, 2018.

AUTHOR'S BIO

I have been seated at the table – rather, more accurately, been seated behind the white men seated at the table and told to hold my tongue – at the launch of some of the most radical new business models of the last century.

I have had a front row seat for every new finance and/or economic theory that came down the pike.

This is a dubious honor. I have watched these same new business models crash and burn, take jobs, destroy families, make ghost towns of cities, compromise our health and well being, and rob us of our happiness. With the economic meltdown of 2008, I watched as my retirement fund plummeted 42% percent from the top of the market in 2007 to the bottom in 2009.

My life has been magical. I have over 70 years life/work experience and an excellent educational background.

Syracuse University (1965) – In my Accounting courses, I learned to fill in forms and play games with numbers. In Anthropology and Public Speaking, I learned storytelling and gained an appreciation of other cultures.

Diane Freaney, photo from *Messages to a President* by Julie Keefe

Harvard Business School – Corporate Finance Executive Education (1982) – I learned about OPM (Other People's Money), the strategy that brought the Global Financial Markets to their knees in 2008.

University of Pennsylvania – Organizational Dynamics (1999) – I learned that student's work is only valued when it follows a structured academic path. My Master's thesis – *A New Model for the Creative Use of College Endowments to Reduce College Tuition* would have prevented today's student loan crisis. Penn had no mechanism for "the administrators" to listen to students.

Bainbridge Graduate Institute (BGI) (2013) – I learned the importance of social media to listening deeply and delivering my message.

At an early age, I learned to communicate by listening. At my current age, I feel driven to share the knowledge and understanding amassed during my lifetime. Now I am speaking out.

— Diane Freaney, The Cat Lady

APPENDICES

Appendix A. Bank of Cattaraugus

"Bank of Cattaraugus hires within for new CEO," by Allisa Klein. Buffalo Business News, March 19, 2019

One of the smallest banks in Western New York will continue as a family operation. Colleen Young will succeed her father, Patrick Cullen, as president and CEO of Bank of Cattaraugus. The tiny bank has a single office in the village of Cattaraugus – about an hour south of Buffalo – and approximately $21 million in assets.

Young joined the bank in 1997 and filled various roles including vice president, director and chief financial officer. She is a graduate of St. Bonaventure University where she studied business and accounting.

Cullen will become chairman of the bank's board of directors. Thirty-seven year ago, he succeeded his own father, L. Edgar Cullen, who had been in charge of the bank for 25 years.

Colleen Young will succeed her father, Patrick Cullen, as president and CEO of Bank of Cattaraugus

Bank of Cattaraugus was founded in 1882. All of its deposits come from Cattaraugus County.

(Used with permission from the Buffalo Business First: https://www.bizjournals.com/buffalo/news/2019/03/19/bank-of-cattaraugus-hires-within-for-new- ceo.html)

"The Bank Around the Corner," by Alan Feuer. New York Times, December 23, 2011

As winter approached, a retired secretary here named Carol Bonner was putting snow tires on her car when she noticed that her back-right rim was bent. Ms. Bonner took the car to Otto's Auto Body Shop and got bad news: the work was going to run her $244 — more than half of her $417 monthly pension check.

Without a credit card or enough saved up to replace the rim herself, Ms. Bonner, who is 61 and cares for her sister Jane, who is disabled, did the only thing she could do: she went down to the Bank of Cattaraugus and took out a $300 loan. The bank, in a reversal of the usual process, had bailed her out before. A few years ago, when Ms. Bonner fell behind on her property taxes and was forced to sell her home, the bank's president, Patrick J. Cullen, who held the mortgage on the house, had his son Thomas buy it. Thomas Cullen, who lives in Chicago, never intended to live there. Ms. Bonner and her sister were able to stay as renters.

Carol Bonner went to the bank recently to obtain a $300 loan for an auto repair. Brendan Bannon for The New York Times

"The whole thing was incredible," Ms. Bonner said the other day, a single pine branch hanging in her living room in lieu of a full Christmas tree, which she could not afford. "I just didn't realize there were people like that in the world, people who would help you.

"Especially," she said, "a banker."

This has not exactly been a time of great love for bankers. Amid the continuing foreclosure crisis and Occupy Wall Street's campaign against "the 1 percent," it is easy to forget that not all banks are complicated giants, trading in derivatives and re-hypothecating valueless collateral. The Bank of Cattaraugus, for example, is by asset size the state's smallest bank (one branch, eight employees, no credit default swaps) and yet it plays an outsize role in this hilly village an hour south of Buffalo: housing its deposits, lending to its neediest inhabitants and recently granting forbearance on a mortgage when the borrower, a bus mechanic, temporarily lost his job after shooting off his finger while holstering his gun.

If it sounds old-fashioned, it is. It's not the kind of bank you'll find anymore in New York City, where multiple branches and capitalizations counted in 10 figures are the norm. With $12 million in total assets, the Bank of Cattaraugus is a microbank, well below the $10 billion ceiling that defines small banks. It exists in a seemingly different universe from the mammoth banks-turned-financial-services-conglomerates, like Citigroup ($1.9 trillion in assets) or JPMorgan Chase ($2.25 trillion).

The Bank of Cattaraugus, as depicted on an overdraft notice. —Brendan Bannon for The New York Times

With obvious exceptions, business at the Bank of Cattaraugus hasn't changed much since 1882, when 20 prominent residents — among them a Civil War surgeon and a cousin of Davy Crockett — established the bank to safeguard townsfolk's money and to finance local commerce.

In its 130-year history, the bank has rarely booked a profit for itself in excess of $50,000. Last year, Mr. Cullen said, it made $5,000. He and his officers are industry anomalies: bankers who avoid high-risk and high-growth tactics in order to reinvest in their community's economy.

"My examiners always ask me, 'When are you going to grow?'" said Mr. Cullen, a Cattaraugus native who is 64 and has the prosperous stoutness of a storybook banker. "But where is it written I have to grow? We take care of our customers. The truth is we probably couldn't grow too much in a town like this."

While it faces many of the same regulations that govern larger banks, it operates according to an antiquated theory of the business: that a bank should be a utility, like the power company, and serve as a broker between savers and borrowers in its community.

Cattaraugus, nestled in the woods of the misleadingly named Rich Valley, is a town of limited prospects. ("We're not on the way to anywhere," Mr. Cullen said.) Manufacturing, which once thrived here, has more or less died — except for the Setterstix factory on South Main Street, which produces paper lollipop handles. The largest employer in the village is the school district, and many village residents survive, like Ms. Bonner, on pensions or government subsidies, in homes that have an average mortgage of $30,000.
Mr. Cullen's bank is the only one in town — the next-closest is in Little Valley, seven miles away.

In this difficult environment, Mr. Cullen — like the bank's former president, his father, L. E. Cullen — occupies a paternal, if not quite paternalistic, position: a well-to-do man who is sufficiently familiar with the local economy that he does not use credit scores when handing out a loan.

"Numbers don't tell the story here," he said one day, relating the tale of an Amish customer who wanted $85,000 to consolidate his debts. Even though the man earned only $2,300 a year — from selling greenhouse starter kits — Mr. Cullen gave him the loan.

"If you know Amish culture, you know his sons work and that everything they earn goes to him until they're 21 or married," Mr. Cullen said, observing that the man had eight sons, each earning at least $10 an hour. "So he was fine, but none of that shows up on a credit score."

Mr. Cullen's first job at the bank was wrapping pennies for his father at age 5. When he was 9, he helped repossess a car. After two years at the Marine-Midland Bank in Buffalo, he joined the family bank as an assistant cashier — he was 24 — and he has been there ever since, commuting each morning to his office on Main Street from his house around the corner: a 20-second drive.

The bank remains a family business. His daughter, Colleen C. Young, is the chief financial officer, and his wife, Joan A. Cullen, is the corporate secretary (she used to keep the books, but it was thought to be improper that the bank auditor slept in the same bed as the president).

A teller, Sandy Allen, served a customer, Michael Eckert, at the Bank of Cattaraugus, which was established in 1882. Brendan Bannon for The New York Times

The Cullens — there are three more children, all sons and all in finance in Chicago — are that oddest of commodities: a beloved banking family.

"They saved our lives," said Duane Kelley, a retired Setterstix worker who, a few years ago, lost the house he lived in with his wife to a $15,000 tax lien. Mr. Cullen bought the house at a county land auction with the bank's money and returned it to the Kelleys. They are paying him back through a 15-year loan.

SMALL banks have been dying for 20 years. In 1990, there were 12,000 banks nationwide with assets of less than $10 billion; now, there are 7,350. The country's top five banks have, meanwhile, grown relentlessly: In 1995, they held 11 percent of all deposits; last year it was 34 percent.

For several years, the small-banking sector has been pinched on one side by the rising costs of compliance and technology, and on the other by historically low interest rates (which cut into lending margins). In the last year, though, anger over big banks' fees and mortgage lending practices has turned consumers against the mega-banks, and smaller institutions have been the beneficiaries.

The publisher Arianna Huffington has been behind the Move Your Money Project, which encourages people to take their money out of big banks and deposit it in local financial institutions. (Slogan: Invest in Main Street, Not Wall Street.) Ms. Huffington produced a video based on the Christmas banking classic "It's a Wonderful Life" to support the campaign. BankTransferDay.org similarly claims to have persuaded 400,000 people to switch their funds from big banks to not-for-profit credit unions. Occupy Wall Street, which has pretty much turned "bank" into a four-letter word, has deposited nearly $500,000 into Amalgamated Bank, a big small bank in New York City owned by the labor union Unite Here.

Edward Grebow, Amalgamated's president, posted signs in his branches supporting the movement and marched with its members in October. Perhaps as a result, the number of new checking accounts at Amalgamated has doubled in the months since it took on Occupy Wall Street as a customer. But the increased business came at a delicate moment for the bank: under new rules passed in the wake of the subprime lending meltdown, Amalgamated was forced to raise fresh capital. In September, the bank sold a 40 percent stake in its business to two giants of the private-equities markets: Wilbur L. Ross Jr., a billionaire investor, and Ronald W. Burkle, a California supermarket magnate. According to Camden R. Fine, the president of the Independent Community Bankers of America, an advocacy group for small banks, nearly every bank regulation of the last 20 years was put in place in response to real or perceived malfeasance by the country's largest banks.

"Community banks are paying for the greed and overreach of the biggest players in the market," he said. "For a small bank in Ashland, Mo., say, it's absurd to apply the body of regulation that a Citicorp has to deal with."

The question facing community banks today is whether their current vogue can offset the abiding trend toward consolidation. Even in Cattaraugus — population 950 — Mr. Cullen says he receives at least two offers a week from larger institutions that want to buy him out. He claims to be unsurprised by these overtures, though his business is exceptionally simple: 80 percent of the loans in his portfolio are mortgages, a third of them arising from marital separation. ("Two people are living together; they split," he said. "Now, instead of one house, you need two.") Still, his answer to potential buyers is always the same: no thanks. "There's nothing they can offer us," he said, "that we can't do ourselves."

The core problem at banks like his is that the comparative advantages they offer — customer service, access to managers, an intimate knowledge of borrowers — do not always translate to the bottom line, even if they do yield dividends in public relations.
"They do things that big banks won't do," said Paul Macakanja, the owner of the Jenny Lee diner, which sits on Main Street facing Mr. Cullen's bank. The diner has no photocopier, and tellers at the bank, he said, will run off copies of his menu, free of charge. "They support you personally," he added, "because your success is their success.

It is for these and other reasons that Mr. Fine argued poignantly on behalf of small banks. They hold 20 percent of the country's assets, he said, and yet write more than half of its small-business loans. "Customers can say, 'I know where my money is — it's down there eight blocks away,'" he said. "They can walk in and talk to the president and know he isn't sucking in their money and betting against them on proprietary securities."

Nonetheless, 400 community banks have disappeared in the last three years.

In 1982, Mr. Cullen published a chapbook to celebrate his bank's centennial. The book contained a photograph of the bank's first president, the elaborately bearded Oscar F. Beach, and another of himself, from childhood, which bore the caption: "Ms. Berger's kindergarten class 1953."

"Banking, as one might imagine, is a very interesting business," he wrote. "In a rural area, it is also a very important business. When customers entrust their life savings to us, we treat it as if it were our own."

Beyond a business, Mr. Cullen sees banking as an instrument — one that can shape and preserve the history of his village, which he cites with an archivist's fluidity. His office is cluttered with local artifacts: a mug from the Third Annual Amish Relief Auction; an old sign reading, "Cattaraugus Chowder & Marching Society." One of his most treasured possessions is a leather map bag that belonged to Theodore Roosevelt, who passed through town during his New York gubernatorial campaign.

For the last six years, Mr. Cullen has owned and operated the American Museum of Cutlery across the street from his bank, which honors Cattaraugus's onetime pre-eminence in the knife-making trade.

Between his day job and his other hobbies — antique firearms, an Irish band — Mr. Cullen runs the Historic Cattaraugus Corporation, a nonprofit business that has purchased several buildings in town (the 1909 theater, the 1915 Ford dealership) and refurbished them and rented them out, or simply stopped them from deteriorating. The idea came to him in 1990, he said, when a schoolteacher left town and simply abandoned his house. Not long after, the garage collapsed.

The property was dangerous enough that the school district would not let students walk by. It was an eyesore; it was dragging property values down. "I went and camped out at his new place, and when he went to work, I said, 'Listen, you can't do this to our community,'" Mr. Cullen recalled. He persuaded the man to deed the house back to the bank. The bank paid for a renovation and eventually resold it — at a loss of only $500, Mr. Cullen said.

From 1990 to 2003, when the historical corporation was formed, Mr. Cullen invested nearly $1 million of the bank's money in properties in the village, often getting it back, but not always. "Banks tend not to do that sort of thing," he stated dryly. (His wife, more succinctly, said, "Growth isn't Patrick's thing.") Now, however, with grants from the state, Mr. Cullen has bought, among other things, the glorious old moldering hotel in town, and he is patiently waiting for an opportunity to put it to use.

The corporation recently acquired Mr. Cullen's most cherished local property: the 4.5-acre plot where Cattaraugus was founded (the same spot where, not coincidentally, the campaigning Teddy Roosevelt addressed townsfolk from the back of a train). Dreaming as only a small-town banker dreams, Mr. Cullen plans to rebuild the original buildings — from the shingle maker's shop to the stagecoach station — and open them to the public as a Colonial Williamsburg-style theme park.

"If you look at Williamsburg's Web site, they claim the park employs 3,800 people," he said. "Give us 5 percent of that, I'll claim success."

Mr. Cullen hints that there is interest in his project among certain personages in Washington — he is a banker, after all, who knows other bankers, who know politicians — but it would contradict the very purpose of the project, he said, to finance it with federal money. Cattaraugans know Cattaraugus. The venture will be locally grown.

"Everyone will be involved," he said. "The bank, the church, local government, the people — everyone will have a stake. Creating that experience is what it means to be American, in a sense. It's what it means to be from a place."

Source: The New York Times, https://www.nytimes.com/2011/12/25/nyregion/the-bank-of-cattaraugus-new-york-states-smallest-bank-plays-an-outsize-role.html A version of this article appears in print on , Section MB, Page 1 of the New York edition with the headline: The Bank on Main Street)

APPENDIX B: COTTONWOOD IN THE FLOOD

Cottonwood in the Flood: a staged reading of a play about Vanport, on May 25th.

Cottonwood in the Flood by Rich Rubin

It is the early 1940s, and the United States has just made its entry into World War II. The country is in dire need of ships and workers to build them. From all corners of the land, thousands flock to the shipyards outside Portland, Oregon in search of good pay and steady work. To house the daily-arriving workers and their families, a new city called Vanport is built on a floodplain of the Columbia River. By late 1943, its population swells to nearly 40,000 men, women and children. Many of these people are from the South and many are African-American. Over the next half-decade, Vanport becomes a cauldron in which America's nobler ideals and America's history of racial injustice uneasily mix.

"Cottonwood in the Flood" focuses on the experiences of a fictional African-American family during Vanport's rise and fall. The life the Hawkins family finds in Vanport is both new and depressingly familiar. Schools and rec halls are integrated, but housing and hospital wards are not. Unions advocate for fair treatment of workers, yet black workers are excluded from membership. The war in Europe uncovers the horrors of the Holocaust while at the same time people in America -- and people in Vanport -- are confronting many of our own troubled ways.

As their hopes are raised and their dreams are dashed, the members of the Hawkins family do their best to adjust to daily life in Vanport and grab hold of their fair slice of the American pie. On Memorial Day 1948, the entire city of Vanport is obliterated by a catastrophic flood of the Columbia River, an event that in several discomfiting respects presages the devastation wrought by Hurricane Katrina nearly six decades later.

(Source: https://newplayexchange.org/plays/56637/cottonwood-flood)

The reading of the play was staged in honor of the 1948 Memorial Day Vanport Flood on May 25th, 2015 at the Westminster Presbyterian Church, 1624 NE Hancock St, Portland, Oregon.

APPENDIX C. FROM MAXVILLE TO VANPORT

Partial program from Portland Jazz Composers Ensemble

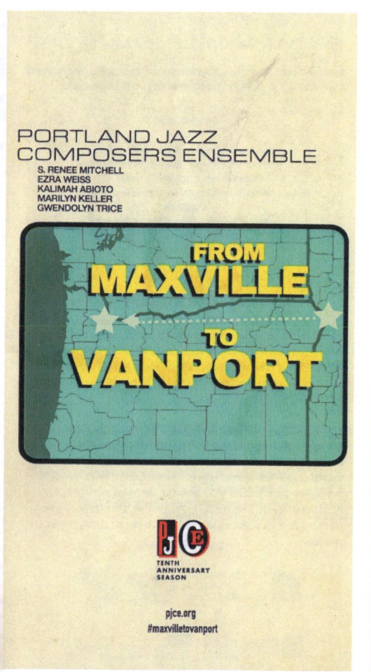

FROM MAXVILLE TO VANPORT

Songs and short films celebrating Oregon history from the perspective of the African American residents of these two unique places.

PROGRAM

Oregon Sounds Like Freedom (Rob Davis, tenor sax)
What Do Your Trees Tell You? (Douglas Detrick, flugelhorn)
Woman's Work (John Moak, trombone)
Marjorie (Mieke Bruggeman, bari sax; Jasnam Daya Singh, piano)
INTERMISSION
Stacked Deck Hand (Farnell Newton, trumpet)
Water
From Maxville to Vanport

Lyrics by S. Renee Mitchell, music by Ezra Weiss, films by Kalimah Abioto, featuring Marilyn Keller, voice. Historical consultation by Gwendolyn Trice.

Performed by the Portland Jazz Composers Ensemble:
Lee Elderton — soprano sax, clarinet; John Savage — alto sax, flute; Rob Davis — tenor sax, clarinet; Mieke Bruggeman — bari sax, bass clarinet; Douglas Detrick and Farnell Newton — trumpet, flugelhorn; John Moak and Denzel Mendoza — trombone; Ryan Meagher — guitar; Jasnam Daya Singh — piano; Bill Athens — bass; Ken Ollis — drums

OREGON TOUR DATES

April 11	2 pm	Groth Hall, Eastern Oregon University, La Grande, OR, masterclass
April 12	1 pm	OK Theatre, Enterprise, OR, performance for Wallowa County students
April 12	7:30 pm	Groth Hall, Eastern Oregon University, La Grande, OR
April 13	1 pm	Josephy Center, Joseph, OR. Improvised performances for art students
April 13	7 pm	OK Theatre, Enterprise, OR
April 14	6 pm	Grand Ballroom, Baker Heritage Museum, Baker City, OR
May 26	7 pm	Alberta Rose Theater, Portland, OR

Thanks to our sponsors

FROM THE ARTISTIC DIRECTOR

Maxville, a logging town built in 1923 in Wallowa County, and Vanport, built in 1942 just north of Portland for shipyard workers, were multicultural communities that housed workforces with significant African American and immigrant populations at a time when many Oregonians were openly hostile to them. From Maxville to Vanport looks honestly at the prejudice these people faced and celebrates their resilience, courage, and important contributions to Oregon. It tells stories of life, liberty, and the pursuit of happiness in the face of remarkable adversity; stories that deserve to be better understood by all Oregonians.

Logging crew at Maxville.

From the beginning of World War I through the 1960s, millions of African American people moved from the South in a mass exodus called the Great Migration. They did so to escape the oppressive conditions of the South, where African Americans were systematically forced into a second-class existence through Jim Crow laws, and lynching was a constant threat. None of these refugees knew exactly what the future would hold for them, but all of them knew that even if life would be better in the North, it still wouldn't be easy. Leaving their homes and communities behind seemed worth the risk, even if the opportunities they pursued were still unequal to those enjoyed by white Americans.

Jazz was a product of the Great Migration, too. This music was created by African American musicians in New Orleans in the early 20th century. Then it was a hyper-local music played only in certain neighborhoods; now it is a wildly diverse music played by all kinds of people all over the world. Louis Armstrong, a black musician and one of jazz's first superstars, moved from New Orleans to Chicago in 1922. There he would make his first recordings, and eventually become one of the world's best-known musicians—achievements he would have been unlikely to attain had he stayed in New Orleans. Even though Armstrong's profession was different, he moved north for the same reasons as did the men and women who cut logs and built ships in Oregon.

Women shipyard workers.

THE MAKING OF FROM MAXVILLE TO VANPORT

The lyrics in From Maxville to Vanport were written by S. Renee Mitchell, the music was written by Ezra Weiss, the short films were directed and produced by Kalimah Abioto, and Douglas Detrick was the artistic director. The project doesn't present a single narrative, but rather is a collection of reactions, contemplations, and commemorations connected to the stories of Maxville and Vanport.

Our artistic team spoke with audiences in Portland and Wallowa County, where we asked the people directly connected to these histories to tell us how they felt about them and how they would want us to portray their experiences. That feedback along with extensive conversations with Maxville Heritage Interpretive Center Executive Director Gwendolyn Trice and other descendants and former residents of both Vanport and Maxville informed the creation of the piece. It was essential for their narratives to be portrayed authentically and respectfully in this project, and we are so grateful to have had so many participate so generously.

THE SONGS AND FILMS OF FROM MAXVILLE TO VANPORT

Oregon is a beacon of hope in the opening song, "Oregon Sounds Like Freedom," where even if life was hard it was better than being "chased by the Klan." In "What Do Your Trees Tell You," the trees themselves take on a new meaning, symbolizing the chance for a brighter future rather than the brutal reality of lynchings in the South.

The contributions of women in Maxville and Vanport were just as vital as the men's. In "Woman's Work," an R&B song reminiscent of those sung by Aretha Franklin, "sleep is like a tourist," a fleeting presence in the lives of the hardworking women of Maxville. In "Marjorie," the film's main character is the wife of a Maxville logger who imagines a different life for herself in the city as a musician. Maxville was in operation from 1921 to 1933, and when the Bowman Hicks lumber company closed the town, some residents stayed while others left, including some who ended up in Vanport decades later. This film imagines what many residents might have been thinking as they faced the prospect of another long winter in Wallowa County.

"Stacked Deck Hand" asks how one can win in cards or life when the deck is stacked against you. It has all the swagger and soul that you expect from a classic blues song, but it also goes deeper, celebrating family, perseverance, and faith.

"Water" is a short film about a boy playing outdoors, like boys who lived in Vanport would have done, climbing and running, playing marbles, tossing a baseball, and boxing. Soon, the boy sees rushing waters that foreshadow the Vanport Flood, and then we see the boy as a man, remembering rather than anticipating the flood of emotions he felt at the loss of his home.

"From Maxville to Vanport," the closing piece of the concert, marvels at how people who gave up everything they had for an uncertain future wound up making history. "Oregon didn't want black folks to stay/ But we planted roots here anyway," the song says. It is that courage that we celebrate in "From Maxville to Vanport".

Thank you for taking part in this process!
Douglas Detrick
Executive Director, Portland Jazz Composers Ensemble

ABOUT THE CREATIVE TEAM

Lyricist S. Renee Mitchell is an award-winning writer and published author, multimedia artist, social justice advocate, and teacher/facilitator. Mitchell's more than 25 years of journalism experience has groomed her exceptional communication, analytical and grant-writing skills, yet, Renee is also a community-grounded visionary. She is the 2015 Yolanda D. King Drum Major Award winner in recognition of dedicated community service; was the librettist of "Sherman: A Jazz Opera;" has published a novel, children's story, and several small-press zines; and teaches writing to children as the leader of the Saturday Academy Social Justice Camp as well as many other Portland institutions.

Composer Ezra Weiss has recorded seven albums as a bandleader, most recently "Before You Know It," recorded live Portland, and composed songs and book for Northwest Children's Theater's "Alice in Wonderland." He has led his own bands at major venues throughout the U.S., including several week-long engagements at Jazz at Lincoln Center's Dizzy's Club. He has won the ASCAP Young Jazz Composer Award three times and has been listed in DownBeat Critics Polls in the Rising Star Arranger category. He currently teaches at Portland State University and holds a Bachelors in Jazz Composition from the Oberlin Conservatory and a Masters in Jazz Piano from Queens College.

Vocalist Marilyn Keller is a singer who performs a diverse range of jazz, gospel, and musical theatre throughout Oregon and abroad and was voted into Oregon Jazz Society's Hall of Fame 2016. She joined Black Swan Classic Jazz Band in 1997 and has toured throughout Europe and the US. She has also remained active in a wide variety of other performance ensembles and styles: The Don Latarski Group, Darrell Grant's The Territory, Thara Memory, Tall Jazz, Disciples in Song, and the Augustana Jazz Quartet among many others.

A native of Memphis, Tennessee, filmmaker Kalimah Abioto began playing the drums at age three, writing in elementary school, and makings films in high school centered around dreams, sexuality, and the nexus between Black people, humans, freedom, and the natural-spirit worlds. She received her BA in film and video from Hollins University and is a co-creator, along with her four sisters of The People Could Fly Project, a multimedia project documenting the dreams and stories of people in the African Diaspora. Abioto has worked with different artists and groups including Afropop Worldwide, Holy Mojo, The Black Portlanders, Spirit Law Center, Diamond Law, and others that value life force. She was a 2017 Artist in Residence at Open Signal.

Historian Gwendolyn Trice founded Maxville Heritage Interpretive Center, a non-profit cultural heritage center in Wallowa County, Oregon and serves as its Executive Director. She also provided support and information for OPB's 2009 video Logger's Daughter. Currently, she serves on the Oregon Commission on Black Affairs and is part of a Leadership cohort for the Center for Diversity and Environment.

THE POETRY OF FROM MAXVILLE TO VANPORT

By S. Renee Mitchell

OREGON SOUNDS LIKE FREEDOM

Oregon sounds like freedom
Sounds like freedom
Freedom
Freedom freedom freedom
Think I'll go

Oregon sounds like freedom
Oregon sounds like freedom
Oregon sounds like freedom
Think I'll go
Think I'll go

had a farm in Alabama
tended corn and peanuts too
but the crop done rot
once the buyers thought
black man is good for only shining shoes

that's what i say
Oregon sounds like freedom
Oregon sounds like freedom
Oregon sounds like freedom
Think I'll go
Think I'll go

my little brother got in some trouble
a pretta white gal promised him fun
but all that fun stopped
when she called the cops
now his horny ass is on run

that's what i say
Oregon sounds like freedom
Oregon sounds like freedom
Oregon sounds like freedom
Think I'll go
Think I'll go

I ain't never been there
but i think it's grand
can't be much worse
than being chased by the Klan
Oregon sounds like freedom
think i'll go
Oregon sounds like freedom
Oregon sounds like freedom
Oregon sounds like freedom
Think I'll go

WOMAN'S WORK

Sleep is like a tourist
who don't know where it belongs
it don't come regular
don't stay too long
I works hard – to keep my household fed
I works hard – to clothe what I have bred
i works hard – my family depends on me
I works hard to make time for everything else but sleep

i rise before the sun plays peek-a-boo
to sizzle him some breakfast; prepare his lunch, too
my logging man needs 6,000 daily calories
my logging man works so hard to take care of me
my logging man brought me here to raise our family
and i'm taking care of bizness til he comes home to me

My tired eyes are the last to shut
but first to open
when it's time to get up
I works hard – to keep my household fed
I works hard to clothe what I have bred
i works hard, my family depends on me
I works hard to make time for doing everything else but sleep

Once he's off in the wagon, I wake the chil'ren up
gotta dress 'em, then i feed 'em the leftover grub
my logging man works so hard, I gotta do my part
chil'ren got me for a stretch, but he's got my heart
got no time for myself, got no time for the blues
got to shoo the young-uns outside, 'cause i got stuff to do

I can jam and I sew
and wouldn't you know
my only time alone
is in the outhouse to pee
I works hard – to keep my household fed
I works hard to clothe what I have bred
I works hard in winter just to stay warm
I stuff walls with paper to keep out the storm
I works hard to wash and hang our blankets on lines
'Cause it takes several days for the wool to dry
I works hard, my family depends on me
I works hard to make time for doing everything else but sleep

WHAT DO YOUR TREES TELL YOU?

The trunks of trees, they call my name.
But the whisperings are not the same.
Branches stretched to give live,
Been used to take life too.
Our nature reveals what nature is purposed to do.
What do your trees tell you? Huh?
What do your trees tell you? Huh?
What do your trees tell you? Huh?
What do your trees tell you?

The place I'm from, the S-'s hiss from your mouth.
The P's hum like a hoarse harmonica.
Mississippi, home of fat back and fried okra,
Fields of white cotton, brown hands, bowed head.
Born there, don't wanna die there.
Leastways not 'fore my time.
But a' times quite frankly
That choice not be mine.

The trunks of trees, they call my name.
But the whisperings are not the same.
Branches stretched to give live,
Been used to take life too.
Our nature reveals what nature is purposed to do.
What do your trees tell you? Huh?
What do your trees tell you? Huh?
What do your trees tell you? Huh?
What do your trees tell you?

Escaped to an oasis called Oregon
By chasing opportunity.
Brought my Delta music, ways and women.
Established new community.
Brought for our skills to help timber thrive.
Escaping Southern trees,
Found Northern trees.
Best way to keep my fam'ly alive.

It's all about your outlook.
Some see death, some opportunity.
A change in perspective does a man's heart good.
Makes all the diff'rence to what he believes.

The trunks of trees, they call my name.
But the whisperings are not the same.
Branches stretched to give live,
Been used to take life too.
Our nature reveals what nature is purposed to do.

From Mississippi to Maxville,
From hanging up to cutting down.
Lives discovered amongst the branches
That speak to journeys profound.
What do your trees tell you? Huh?
What do your trees tell you? Huh?
What do your trees tell you? Huh?
What do your trees tell you?

Appendix D: The ADU at the Emerson Street House

What Is an Accessory Dwelling Unit (ADU)?

Investopedia defines ADU as:

"An accessory dwelling unit (ADU) is a legal and regulatory term for a secondary house or apartment that shares the building lot of a larger, primary home. The unit cannot be bought or sold separately, but they are often used to provide additional income through rent or to house a family member. For example, an elderly parent could live in a small unit and avoid having to move to an assisted living facility."

ADU Study by the Oregon Department of Environmental Studies

Lina Minard, Niche Consulting founder/owner/operator, Whitman College, Class of 2005, was evidently hired by the Oregon Department of Environmental to conduct a study of ADU in Portland Oregon. This is ADU Case Study that I submitted to Lina.

The ADU at the Emerson Street House
Quick Facts
Setting: Urban – Northeast Portland
Neighborhood: King Neighborhood, Northeast Portland, OR
Type: New Construction – Main House and ADU
ADU Use: Diane Freaney's Live/Work/Studio Space
Square Footage: 798 SF
Year Built: Certificate of Occupancy Issued May 2, 2016
Owner: Emerson Street House LLC, an Oregon Benefits Company, single-member Diane Freaney
Designer: Jeff Stern, In Situ Architecture, Certified Passive House Consultant
Original Builder: Original Design Build Firm has resigned from the project
Original Builder Cost: $376,325.70 ($471.59 per SF)
Replicable Cost: $160,000 ($200.00 per SF)

In June 2013, Diane graduated from Bainbridge Graduate Institute (BGI) (now merged with Presidio) with an MBA in Sustainable Systems. The second-year curriculum changed the focus of Diane's work from Wall Street investing to rooted investing – Local Living Economies (Stuart Cowan), Green Build (Jason McLennan), Energy (Jimmy Jia) and Food and Agriculture (John Gardner).
After graduation, Diane connected with Lise and Steve Monohan, goat farmers from Gales Creek, Oregon. Lise wrote to BGI asking for help in securing financing for a new dairy barn. Lise and Steve purchased Fraga Farms,

a well-respected local goat cheese maker. The Fraga goats had to be moved from Sweet Home, Oregon to Gales Creek. The local bank turned Lise and Steve down for a $100,000 loan. Their farm appraised at $500,000, with a $90,000 mortgage, a 15-year mortgage AND they had never missed a payment. Lise had a full-time job as a public health nurse. AND Lise and Steve owned 3 investment properties, single-family homes in Portland, all rented at below market rates, which more than covered the mortgage payment, including real estate taxes and insurance.

Lise and Steve decide to sell their property in the Alberta Arts district. They purchased 1006 NE Emerson Street on May 2, 2005, with a 15-year mortgage. The tenant had already given notice that she was moving out at the end of the lease.

Diane just sold all her Wall Street investments and had cash to make local investments. Diane and Lise agreed on a price and closed in August. Lise taught Diane about tiny houses, Accessory Dwelling Units (ADUs), Portland building codes, the history of North and Northeast Portland and the King neighborhood.

Diane's goal was to build at least 2 living units on the property. Diane had a lot to learn and many false starts. She had plans drawn up to renovate the existing house and put a tiny house on the property. Then a renovation and a free standing ADU. Finally, Diane learned there was no other option except to deconstruct the existing structure and start from scratch – the original foundation was built without rebar and the house was riddled with black mold.

Jeff Stern, It Situ Architecture, gave Diane a tour of Skidmore Passivhaus, his family's home, studio, and office in the Cully neighborhood. Jeff built Skidmore Passivhaus using Passive house standards. The building is placed on the property to take maximum advantage of the sun to provide heat in cold months, electric shades to keep the sun out during hot months, thick heavily insulated walls, tight envelope, cement floors, special doors and windows.

Diane decided to build a Passive House, Net Zero house with an attached ADU after her tour of Skidmore Passivhaus. The studio and office wing has a bathroom that Diane replicated in the Emerson Street House. There is currently no kitchen in the studio and office wing so Skidmore Passivhaus is not classified as an ADU. A kitchen could be added if living needs changed.

Smaller spaces, less stuff, shared spaces, and spaces that serve multiple purposes create sustainable, resilient communities. The Emerson Street House was designed to serve many purposes, for now and over time.

The ADU layout is simple – approximately 36' x 25' exterior walls, 798 SF, with 2 bedrooms, 1 bath and a "great room" that includes a kitchen, laundry, living space, studio, and office.

Inspirations for the project were Jane Jacobs, *The Death and Life of Great American Cities*; Annie Leonard, *The Story of Stuff*; and Theaster Gates, Artist, based on the south side of Chicago. Diane – "My goal was to create community, not just build a building."

To finance the project, Diane reinvested funds from the sale of her condo and used personal funds formerly invested in Wall Street to pay for the balance. Diane's philosophy, **owning your own home, free of any debt, is the best investment anyone can make.** Learn how to maintain your home and your home will maintain its value. When your mortgage is paid off, consider adding an ADU and renting it out either on a nightly/weekly basis or affordably to local resident(s) (30% of cash net income for rent and utilities).

Jeff Stern performed the Passive House calculations using the Passive House Planning Package (PHPP), a giant Excel spreadsheet developed by the *Passivhaus Institut* in Germany. The PHPP allows energy modeling and optimization in design. Jeff Stern skill in PHPP modeling gave the Emerson Street House the SIMPLE and structurally efficient design in both the ADU and the MAIN house.

Diane recommends that you hire an independent Architect, even if you will be doing the work yourself. The University of Oregon (UofO) and Portland State University (PSU) both have Architecture programs and may be able to connect you with an Architecture student, if you are concerned about cost.

Nicholas Papaefthimiou, https://www.pdx.edu/architecture/profile/nicholas-papaefthimiou, Adjunct Faculty, PSU and UofO, also builds ADUs which he rents affordably through his company Infill PDX, http://infillpdx.com/who.html.

Diane recommends that you be your own Project Manager for your ADU. The Google definition – "As the project manager, your job is to plan, budget, oversee and document all aspects of the specific project you are working on." The project manager assigned by the builder did not understand his job and the project suffered.

Don't waste time or money on Certifications. Certification is the attempt to verify that a project meets a standard. Earth Advantage issued a Net Zero Certificate dated May 2016, based on a blower test performed in March 2016. The cost of the Certification was $2,700, paid for by "Contractor's Incentive." Earth Advantage only deals with builders AND has refused to meet with Diane.

The best way to record energy data for energy usage for your ADU every month, pay attention to the usage. [Energy Usage Table]. The Emerson Street House ADU is "Net Zero", while the MAIN house is not. Diane, A&R Solar, and a new electrician are diagnosing the situation, with a goal of reaching Net Zero for both the MAIN House and the ADU to meet "Net Zero" standards for the Living Building Challenge of the International Living Future Institute.

The Passive House Institute US (PHIUS) issued a Certificate, dated August 1, 2016, which indicates to Diane that Jeff Stern completed the Certification at the Emerson Street House on August 1, 2016. The Emerson Street House did not meet *Passivhaus Institut* standards that August 1, 2016. The inside temperature was 80 degrees, with still air, no ventilation.

Major design considerations. Diane is 73 years old with Charcot-Marie-Tooth, a neurological disease that affect Diane's strength, balance, and mobility. The ADU is Diane's live/work space, where Diane plans to live and work for the rest of her life.

1. Diane's requirement for no stairs to access the ADU and no stairs inside.

2. Diane wants the ADU to be a public space, where neighbors felt comfortable stopping by and a private space when Diane needs "alone time." The Great Room is visible from the ADU front door. Diane's bedroom, which has a door, is behind the kitchen wall for privacy.

3.   Diane is prone to seasonal depression during the dark days of winter. High ceiling and windows without window covering allow maximum light.

4.   Diane loves Jane Jacobs concept of "eyes on the street." Place a window facing the street where the resident will stand frequently, for example the kitchen. The resident will watch the coming and going of folks, including children, and become an unofficial "safe streets program". Diane wanted the ADU front window to allow Diane to see the street. The window is set too high so Diane has to stand outside the front door to see the street. This is high on Diane's list to correct.

The Emerson Street House, both MAIN house and ADU, was designed for multi-generational living and Aging at Home. Diane's inspiration came from her parent's end of life residency in Assisted Living. The primary caregivers - Certified Nursing Assistants (CNAs) were primarily young mothers. Every morning the CNAs left their children with neighbors, family or friends and drove to the Assisted Living facility, carpooling with neighbors if possible. The CNAs spent the day with cranky, bored old people, with little to look forward to, all the while worrying about their own children.

Diane's parents hated Assisted Living and only wanted to be in their own home. Diane thought – what if houses were designed to allow caregivers and their families to live in a residence with the folks they took care of. The Main house was designed with a master bedroom on the first floor, with an accessible bathroom right outside the bedroom door. Upstairs there are two bedrooms, one bath, a sitting area and access to the roof patio and the eco-roof.

Diane reasons that a senior who wants to stay in their home could trade room and board with a young family. The partners could arrange for one partner to be at home as needed by the senior. The partners would cook, clean, and do laundry for the senior as part of their daily routine of caring for their own family. One partner (or both if they had different schedules) could work outside the home, keeping all earnings to provide for their own families, perhaps saving to purchase their own home in the future.

Diane plans to live in the ADU until she passes. The second bedroom would be available for a caregiver to live-in if Diane needs help. Caregivers could work together to give each more freedom to spent time with their families.

The quality of life for the seniors improves when they stay in their homes with the things they love and their memories AND they have the social life and connection they need because they are part of a young family's life. The reality is that this type of arrangement happens all the time in low-income families because low-income families can't afford Assisted Living.

If Diane had it to do over again, there are seven things Diane would do differently.

1.   Diane would hire an independent Architect. Diane would meet with the Architect weekly, either in person or on Skype or cell, during the planning, permitting, and building stage. Then quarterly for at least two years after the Certificate of Occupancy is issued to diagnose and correct construction defects, if any.

2.   Diane would visit the Bureau of Development Services with the Architect so she understood the permitting process, code issues and how to advocate for her own ideas.

3.   Diane would insist on Hammer & Hand's project model of Three Advocates https://hammerand-hand.com/about/designer-builder-client/a collaborative process between Architect, Builder and Client to design and construct the best response to the project's program.

4.   Diane would follow her rooted investing philosophy – DO IT YOURSELF (DIY) - and act as Project Manager.

5.   Diane would insist on copies of all documentation on the project, including all materials used, original bids from each sub-contractor, all change orders, copies of all bills, and verification of payments, before paying each progress billing.

6.   Diane would assemble her own Home Manual, containing all Maintenance Manuals, documentation of materials used, all accounting documentation from every subcontractor and anything else pertinent to the ADU.

7.   Finally, in any building project there can and will be mistakes. The mark of true professionals is how they craft a solution. Diane would make sure she asked about failures and how the professional handled the failure. Diane would NOT sign a contract with a builder or architect that said they never had a failure or blamed someone else for their failure.

So, what advice does Diane have for homeowners considering creating an ADU on their own property?

Take a DIY approach, even if you will not be doing the building yourself.

Read *Rise: How A House Built a Family* by Cara Brookins. Cara and her four children built a five-bedroom house, using YouTube instructional videos and occasional additional help that seemed to show up at critical times. The one "professional" Cara hired – a licensed and bonded electrician – created more problems that they (both men) solved.

Talk to friends, colleagues and acquaintance who have built and ask about their experience.
Go on ADU tours and just walk around your neighborhood, looking to see if you can spot already existing ADUs. Talk to your neighbors. Ask them how they like ADUs in their neighborhood – or do they even notice.

Be clear about your values and your reasons for building an ADU. For example, Airbnb might seem like a cash cow, until you understand that you are a host, which takes time, and your UNIT may be empty in winter months. Perhaps renting a family at 30% of their income for rent and utilities, will be a better option, if the family will provide maintenance for the ADU and the garden.

E-mail thecatlady@dianefreaney.com to schedule a tour of the ADU at the Emerson Street House. Diane made many mistakes AND she is happy to share her mistakes and her solutions to correct the construction defects.

Other possible things to include:

How do the residents of the ADU and main house interact?

Right now, the MAIN house operates as a community space with an Artist-In-Residency program, the Nikki Brown Clown Free Library, House Concerts, an Art Gallery, and community meetings and events. Donovan Smith, DIY Artist-In-Residency Program Director lives in one of the 3 rooms, with the other two rooms available for Artists.

Diane lives in the ADU with Daphne, her grand dog, a 13-year-old Wheaten Terrier. Diane and Donovan usually meet daily to catch up and perhaps share a meal. Both live and work in the same space so there are business and personal reasons to interact.

Do you feel you have adequate storage in your ADU?

Kitchen – The builder installed kitchen was so poorly designed, Diane was forced to think about kitchens differently. Diane realized that she was only using the oven as a toaster, which heated up the already overheated ADU. And if the oven went away, there was no need for a Hood, which took up precious wall space needed for shelves. The Induction Cooktops never worked and there was no need for a Garbage Disposal because Diane composts.

Diane made an appointment with the kitchen planning department at IKEA, which Diane discovered is THE go-to place for kitchens today. Diane uninstalled both the ADU and the MAIN builder installed kitchens, ordered, and installed IKEA kitchens that cost 10% of the cost of builder installed kitchens, tripled the storage space, and left room to include the washer/dryer and a recycling center in the kitchen footprint.

Closets - The only purpose for closets with doors is to hide the mess. In an ADU, which has a smaller footprint, closet doors also get in the way and make the space seem even smaller. A sustainable solution is to have everything neatly stored in plain sight on shelves and/or hanging on racks. Everything that doesn't fit goes in the free box on the sidewalk. Both IKEA and Storables have inexpensive closet systems that work well.

Diane's only regret is that the builder did not listen when Diane told them that she did NOT want closets at all. "Closets in bedroom are code," said the builder. Diane's response - "The code is outdated. How do we change the code?"

The electrical and the plumbing subcontractors seemed to be confused by the closets also because we found electric wires and plumbing pipes in the strangest places.

What sustainability features were included?

Solar panels on the roof, permeable cement on the driveway, an eco-roof on the MAIN house, and many more. Diane is still working to get complete documentation on materials used from the original Design Build firm and will share complete information as soon as it is available.

Diane is drawn to the philosophy of the International Living Future Institute…

What if every single act of design and construction made the world a better place?

The Living Building Challenge is the world's most rigorous proven performance standard for buildings. People from around the world use our regenerative design framework to create spaces that, like a flower, give more than they take.

ILFI's Seven Petals are PLACE, EQUITY, HEALTH & HAPPINESS, BEAUTY & INSPIRATION and materials, energy, and water. The Emerson Street Team has focused on the Petals all in Caps, the People-Oriented Petals. People, not buildings, create sustainability through creativity, curiosity, and behavior.

There is no one right answer for using materials, energy, and water sustainably. The best sustainability solution right now is a stepping stone to a better solution in the future. Our world is a system and constantly changing as systems do. The only truly detrimental action to creating a sustainable project is "status quo."
The Emerson Street House is registered for the Living Building Challenge and the Emerson Street Community, a neighborhood collective, is registered for the Living Community Challenge, two programs of the International Living Future Institute.

How well is the ADU serving your needs?

Diane loves living in the ADU. She unlocks the door in the morning and has a stream of neighbors and business appointments in and out all day long. The ADU is the perfect space to support her work with rooted investing, connecting local organizations and Oregonians with local investing opportunities. The best way to serve the local community is to become part of the community. Too often we look to outside experts for guidance, when the answers are within ourselves and our communities.

What has surprised you about having an ADU on your property?

The most common question about the Emerson Street House – What is this place?

What do you like best about having an ADU on your property?

All aspects of my life are integrated. I am rooted in my neighborhood for the first time in my life.

What's your favorite feature of your ADU? What are you most proud of?

Great windows and doors that provide good light even in the darkest days of winter. The ADU provides enough privacy by the way it sits on the property so that shades and drapes in the winter are not necessary.

Do you have a website detailing your experience?

Check out the What Is This Place? book series on Diane's Amazon Author's Page www.amazon.com/author/dianefreaney

My web site is www.dianefreaney.com

Anything else you'd like to share?

Portland has many creative, inspiring folks and organizations working to build sustainable, resilient communities. The Emerson Street House is honored to be participating in that process.

APPENDIX E. OREGON'S BLATANT RACISM

When Portland banned blacks: Oregon's shameful history as an 'all-white' state
By DeNeen L. Brown, The Washington Post, June 7, 2017

In 1844, all black people were ordered to get out of Oregon Country, the expansive territory under American rule that stretched from the Pacific coast to the Rocky Mountains.

Those who refused to leave could be severely whipped, the provisional government law declared, by "not less than twenty or more than thirty-nine stripes" to be repeated every six months until they left.

Oregon Country's provisional government, which was led by Peter Burnett, a former slaver holder who came west from Missouri by wagon train, passed the law in 1844 — 15 years before Oregon became a state. The law allowed slave holders to keep their slaves for a maximum of three years. After the grace period, all black people — those considered freed or enslaved — were required to leave Oregon Country. Black women were given three years to get out; black men were required to leave in two.

The law became known as the "Peter Burnett Lash Law." Burnett, who also opposed Chinese migration to Oregon Country, would later become the first American governor of California.

The "Lash Law" was quickly amended and then repealed.

No black people were ever lashed under the law. But the act would become the first of three "exclusion laws" that shaped the Pacific Northwest, banning any additional black people from coming to Oregon Country. Those laws created what one African American professor calls "a very hostile environment" that has long made Oregon and its largest city, Portland, a stronghold for white supremacists like Jeremy Joseph Christian, the man accused of killing two men and severely wounding another on a light-rail train last month.

Few people are aware of Oregon's history of blatant racism, including its refusal to ratify the 14th and 15th Amendments of the Constitution.

In 1848, the territorial government passed a law making it illegal for any "Negro or Mullatto" to live in Oregon Country. In 1850, under the Oregon Donation Land Act, "whites and half breed Indians" were granted 650 acres of land from the government. But any other person of color was excluded from claiming land in Oregon. In 1851, Jacob Vanderpool, the black owner of a saloon, restaurant and boarding home, was actually expelled from Oregon territory.

"The exclusion laws were primarily intended to prevent blacks from settling in Oregon, not to kick out those who were already here," according to Salem Public Library records. But Vanderpool's neighbor "reported him for the crime of being black in Oregon, and Judge Thomas Nelson gave him thirty days to leave the territory."

In 1857, as Oregon sought to become a state, it wrote the exclusion of blacks into its constitution: "No free negro or mulatto, not residing in this State at the time of the adoption of this constitution, shall ever come, reside, or be within this State, or hold any real estate, or make any contract, or maintain any suit therein; and the Legislative Assembly shall provide by penal laws for the removal by public officers of all such free negroes and mulattoes, and for their effectual exclusion from the State, and for the punishment of persons who shall bring them into the State, or employ or harbor them therein."

When Oregon entered the Union in 1859 — it did so as a "whites-only" state. The original state constitution banned slavery, but also excluded nonwhites from living there.

"Oregon is the only state in the United States that actually began as literally whites-only," said Winston Grady-Willis, director of Portland State University's School of Gender, Race and Nations. "Even though there was subsequent legislation that challenged those statutes, the statutes were not removed from the books until 1922."

Grady-Willis added: "It's really important for folks to understand this notion of Oregon as this lily-white state sets the tone and is important structurally for the remainder of history of not only the state, but cities like Portland as well."

Portland's reputation as a progressive city is largely a myth, he said. Portland remains the whitest, large city in United States. According to a July 2015 Census report, the city of 612,206 people, was 77.6 percent white; and 5.8 percent black. Grady-Willis called it "a key site for Klan activity."

This is the historical backdrop for the charges against Christian, 35, who allegedly verbally abused two women on the train, including one wearing a hijab, and then attacked the men who came to their aid.

During a brief court hearing Tuesday, Christian was unapologetic:

"You call it terrorism," Christian said in court. "I call it patriotism."

Oregon has a defiant history of resisting federal laws that gave black people rights.

Karen Gibson, associate professor in Portland State's Toulan School of Urban Studies and Planning, said Oregon rescinded its initial ratification of the 14th Amendment to the U.S. Constitution, which granted citizenship to "all persons born or naturalized in the United States," including former slaves.

Oregon was one of just six states that refused to ratify the 15th Amendment, which gave black men the right to vote. Oregon did not ratify the 15th amendment until 1959 — one hundred years after the state joined the Union. It was a symbolic adoption as part of its centennial celebration. It did not re-ratify the 14th amendment until 1973.

"Many of the white settlers who came here came for the Oregon Land Donation Act. This place was intentionally settled by whites for whites," Gibson said.

"They did not want slavery here. They didn't want land taken over by large plantations so they didn't have to compete with bonded labor. But they also thought blacks were inferior. That is still here. White supremacy is about that: the beliefs that whites were supreme."

Darrell Millner, professor emeritus in Portland State's Black Studies Department, said many early Oregon settlers were opposed to slavery "not because of what it did to blacks but because of what it did to them. Slavery represented a competition they did not wish to work against."

Millner said Oregon became a place where "many practices we associate with the Jim Crow South were legal here." In the 1920s, Oregon had the largest Ku Klux Klan organization west of the Mississippi River. In 1922, Walter Pierce, a member of the Ku Klux Klan, was elected governor of Oregon. Pierce served as a member of the U.S. House of

Representatives from 1932 to 1942.

Oregon's hostility toward blacks remains part of the state's culture.

"In the 1980s and '90s, Oregon became a destination for the largest skinhead movement in the country," Millner said. "Their objective was to achieve something pioneers tried to achieve here and that was to create a white homeland."

Millner said that in the 1980s and 1990s, "in Oregon and especially in Portland, it was very dangerous to be a person of color.

An infamous racial attack occurred in Portland in 1988, when an Ethiopian immigrant was fatally beaten by three white supremacists skinheads on the streets of Portland. Mulugeta Seraw was a student at Portland State University. He was killed by three white supremacists who were members of the White Aryan Resistance who beat him with a baseball bat.

In 1990, the Southern Poverty Law Center and the Anti-Defamation League won a lawsuit against the White Aryan Resistance on behalf of Seraw's family.

Millner said he has lived in Oregon 47 years. When he heard about the stabbings on the train last month he said he was disturbed but not surprised.

"It reinforced the subterranean awareness all people of color in Oregon have that something like that could happen to them at any time and in place," he said. "That is reflective of what people of color in Oregon live with. It is on a subconscious level daily. You are constantly aware that is a possibility."

APPENDIX F. VANESSA WHITE, GENEALOGY RESEARCHER

Vanessa White, Genealogy Researcher

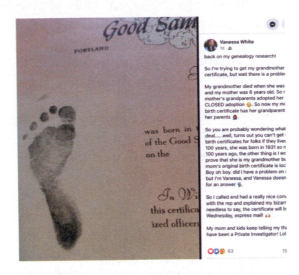

Vanessa White is a neighbor of the Emerson Street House, a serial entrepreneur, a mother, grandmother and one of the smartest, most passionate women I know. Vanessa posts her genealogy research on Facebook.

In one post Vanessa puts down a new headstone for her fourth great grandmother, Jeannette Smith Perry—born in Canada in 1846, and passed away in Oregon in 1891.

WOW! Vanessa's family has been in Oregon for a very long time, long before the migration of southern black folks to Maxville in 1923 and Vanport in 1942.

Appendix G. Black History Month Movers and Shakers

Black History Month movers and shakers, Donald Rodrigue, Feb 3, 2022.

The Hometown News spotlights Stuart Commissioner Eula Clarke

STUART – While some Martin County citizens may think Eula Clarke first came to the limelight upon being elected to the Stuart City Commission here in 2011, the truth is the municipal planner turned lawyer-turned politician has been shaking things up in South Florida since she first arrived in Belle Glade from her native Jamaica when she was 18 years old.

Raised in an upper middle-class family dedicated to hard-work values in that Caribbean nation, she got her first glimpse of stark poverty in Palm Beach County where she still fondly recalls studying with a melting pot of African-American, Mexican-American and Middle-Eastern students. The then-Miss Eula R. Robinson honed her own hard-work ethic after school most days working in the retail stores run by Arab and Palestinian families in Belle Glade.

"I pretty much did what I had to do to move forward," she said. "That included a lot of studying and keeping my eyes on the prize, which was to get a scholarship to a university to avoid my parents having to pay huge school fees. I received the Marshall Hamilton Scholarship upon graduation from Palm Beach Junior College-Glades Armory Campus and went on to Florida State University in the winter of 1978."

As an immigrant youth growing up in the United States, she says she can't recall experiencing racism except for noticing separate treatment of Blacks and always having "to fill out papers with race as one detail." That just served to motivate the young Jamaican even more.

"I just went about my business working to improve myself and set an example for my younger brothers and sisters," she continued. "If someone was ever rude to me in a store, I considered it being rude and not racism. That was my perspective at the time. I learned to ignore a lot of things and just kept pushing forward."

And push forward she did. After graduating with a master of science in urban and regional planning from Florida State University in 1981, she went to work at the City of Ocala the following year, where she spent three years doing transportation planning for the Ocala/Marion County Metropolitan Planning Organization. In 1985, she accepted a position with Martin County as a senior planner in the Growth Management Department where she helped coordinate comprehensive long-range planning. During that same time period, she met and married Dennis Clarke, a Local 728 master electrician with whom she subsequently raised two sons. Ever the consummate student, Mrs. Clarke grew bored with success as a planner and enrolled at the University of Florida where she earned her law degree in 1996. After passing the Florida Bar exam, she briefly opened her own Stuart law office before joining the Florida Rural Legal Services team in 1998 as a family attorney in Fort Pierce working with victims of domestic violence. After litigating more than 100 cases for the organization, she again moved on, first working for a season with the U.S. Census Bureau and then for a Royal Palm Beach law firm before returning to her own private practice in 2002. Over the ensuing decade, she served on more than two dozen volunteer boards as her sons were educated in Martin County public schools. While the eldest son Hugh followed in his mother's legal footsteps and now works as an attorney in Washington D.C., the youngest, Chad, joined the U.S. Army in 2013 after graduating from the University of North Florida and is currently serving as a warrant ogcer at Fort Rucker where he's training to become a helicopter pilot.

Never one to let the grass grow under her feet, Mrs. Clarke again got career restless as Hugh was finishing up his undergraduate degree at the University of Florida. By the time he earned his degree in criminology she had already won her first term as a Stuart City Commissioner in January 2011. Now serving in that capacity for more than a decade, Commissioner Clarke says her biggest challenge over the last 10 years has been ensuring her constituents are kept in the loop of local government and don't feel isolated from the decision-making process.

"Residents are always saying that they did not know about a meeting or event and feel left out while seeking a way to participate," she said. "We have to work hard with innovative ways to ensure they are getting information, and more importantly, that they are providing input as we make decisions."

Her biggest success as a local elected official is communication, a guiding attribute that has characterized her since her youthful days in Belle Glade and still helps her succeed as a lifelong learner.

"My open-door policy and my willingness to go out into all parts of the community and meet with residents is a very important part of being an effective commissioner," she explained.

When asked by the Hometown News if she thought she and her family have had to work harder as African-Americans to prove themselves worthy of success, Ms. Clarke said she couldn't compare herself and her family to others because she didn't know how hard the other people were working.

"I just know that we have standards and expectations and some basic rules about learning all you can – while you can – and doing the best you can with what you have," she said of her family's creed. "Obeying your parents and being respectful of others, etc. That sums up a total effort of always moving forward and not letting obstacles stand in your way, especially when you are healthy and are able to learn and do certain things. It would be like going against the will of God to not do the best you can or at least try."

Mrs. Clarke concluded her comments with her favorite maxim to live by penned by English Poet John Donne in the 17th Century and made famous in song by Joan Baez in 1968. "No man is an island, no man stands alone; each man's joy is joy to me, each man's grief is my own," she wrote. "We need one another, so I will defend each man as my brother, each man as my friend."